The Mended Heart

Diana Douglas

Copyright © 2021 Diana Douglas
All Rights Reserved

Artwork for this book
was done by:

Katelyn Saunders

Dedicated to everyone whose path has crossed mine. Without them, I wouldn't be the person that I am today. Thank you, God for making life so beautiful.

Prologue: The Planted Seed

As we think of the complexities of life, we need to reflect on the past, and prepare for the future. We need to reflect on the past and learn from it. Without reflecting on what has happened, the world keeps playing the same sad tune. When we reflect on the past and learn from it, then we the people grow and start preparing for the future. It's encouraged to reflect on the past, but we must not turn the past into a home. We have to take the past and apply what has been learned to the present. The future is unclear, and we don't know what will happen in the future but taking the knowledge we have and applying it to everyday life it allows us to prepare for the unknown.

We the people are like the flowers and trees of the world. Failure, and struggle are the fertile soil we need in order to help us grow and blossom in the wonderful gifts of life. When life gets tough, and when it seems like it's impossible for things to get better, giving up might seem like the way to go, but it truly isn't. The plants of the world go through seasons just like us, and they come back even stronger after the fall of winter. Make the most out of each day, and let your failures lead you to the success that has always been yours. Life is full of endless possibilities, keep dreaming and allow your heart to lead you home! Home is where your heart leads you. When life seems complex or hard, know that you can get through anything you put your mind to.

List of Poems

Letters to My Guardian Angel 3
The Final Hours 6
When I'm Gone 6
The Key 7
The Weeping Heart 7
Tear Filled Raindrops 8
Hero 10
Messages from the Sky 11
The Spooked Horse 14
Hidden 14
The Quiet Poet 15
Shine 17
A Life Brand New 18
Suffering in Silence 19
Writing Everything Down 20
The Angel's Lesson 21
This Is Your Sign 23
Forever Holding Hands 24
Giving It All To God 25
Day and Night 27
Finally Home 28
Imperfection 28
Blood 29
Fish Out of Water 29
Am I 30
Finding Peace on the Mountain 31

The Waltz	32
God's Blessings	33
TRUE LOVE NEVER DISAPPEARS	34
The Small Puppet	35
Words vs. Actions	37
Honesty	38
Air	38
Motivation	38
The Song of Life	39
Footprints	39
The House of Tears	40
The Last Petal	42
Vision	42
Reminders	43
Blessings In Disguise	44
One More Chance	48
Trust	48
Wings	49
Heaven's Door	49
The Shield of Protection	50
Roots, Branches, and Leaves	52
Masquerade	53
The Sorrow In My Heart	54
The Listening Heart	55
A Voice In The Wind	56
Holding On	58
They Told Me So	59
Living Life in the Blues	59
The Call of Tears	60
The Missing Piece of My Heart	61

The Different Levels of Pain 63
God Called Me Home 64
World Peace 65
Empty Promises 66
The Lost Heartbeat 67
Goodbye Darkness 68
The Golden Heart 69
A Stained Glass Window 70
Suicidal Thoughts 71
Moment by Moment 72
A Christmas Eve Prayer 73
The Lord and The Lighthouse 76
The Porch Swing 77
A Winter Wonderland Holiday 78
The Two Become One 80
My Love For Jesus 81
The Stars In His Eyes 82
The World is Our Home 83
The Unseen Future 84
Creating Connections Through Questions 85
Wandering Thoughts 87
The Broken Heart and Injured Soul 88
Life Requires A Rainstorm 89
A Limited Supply of Time 90
The Warning Signs 91
A Lifetime of Memories 92
The Past Meets the Future 93
The Landfill 94
Unexpected Events 95
Get Out Before it's too Late 96

A Thief's Punishment	97
The Speed Limit	98
Quilts	99
Fear and Regret	100
The Memory Box	101
The Chances Were Given	102
A Cry For Help	103
The Heart that's in Pain	104
The Silent Rush	105
Pacing Back and Forth	106
An Adventure in the Sky	107
The End	108
The Grieving Process	109
Life's Achievements	110
The Homeless Heart	115
Sacrifices	116
Time Creates Our Memories	117
The Lost Soul	118
The Heart and The Clock	119
Finding Rest	120
I Only Want What's Best For You	121
The Light that Shines	122
The Holiday Season	123
When Home is Found	124
The Thankful Glimpse	125
One Life Left to Live	126
The Fragile Heart	127
Take My Heart	128
The Puzzle of Life	129
Letting Love Find You	130

The Last Day	131
Escaping the Cold	132
The Choice Is Yours	133
Forever Dancing Together	134
The Final Hug	135
I Asked God Why	136
Washing Away the Pain	138
The Bells That Ring	139
The Life That Is Given	140
A New Beginning	141
The Key of Life	142
Believe	143
Tending the Garden	144
The Tears of Remembrance	145
The Carolers Message	146
The Lifestyle	147
The Pain that Lingers	148
The Decorated Town	149
A Life Above the Clouds	150
When Fear Takes Over	151
A Dance in Heaven	152
Celebrating Forever	153
The Agenda	155
A Decision for the Lord and Me	156
A Smile Meets the Storm	157
Who I'm Meant To Be	158
Hope Begins to Bloom	159
Going Separate Ways	160
An Angel on Earth	161
A Life of Comprehension	162

A Families Love	163
A World of Inspiration	164
Questioning Life	165
Holding Onto Hope	166
A Wandering Mind	167
Uncovering the Truth	168
When Bedtime Arrives	169
The Silent Scream	170
Making A Wise Decision	171
A Journey to the Light	172
Life's Luxuries	173
Finding a Place to Hide	174
The Transformation	175
Messages from the Heart	176
True Love's Embrace	177
The Homely House	178
Locked Out	179
Stress Relief	180
The Light in my Heart	181
A Never Ending Love	182
A Wounded Warrior	183
The Hopeful World	184
My Brain and Its Thoughts	185
True Love Will Never End	186
The Symphony of Life	187
A Garden of Hope	188
A Love That Remains	189
The Daily Chapter	190
A Gift From God	191
See You Soon	192

The Moon and The Sun	193
Our Love Story	194
Joining Jesus In Heaven	195
The Warrior In Your Heart	196
We Came A Long Way	197
Invisible	198
Facing Reality	200
Get Back Up	201
Taking A Breath of Fresh Air	202
The Remembrance Candle	204
Speechless	205
The Struggling Soul	206
Our Life	207
We Mustn't Forget	208
A Heart With A Wish	209
A Poem to the Love of My Life	210
Signs From Heaven	212
Try	213
First To Last	214
Is Love Blind?	215
Heaven Called	216
A Story Left Behind	217
The Key to My Heart	219
The Past Meets Today	221
Look to The Stars	222
Colliding Hearts	223
Memorial Day	224
One Day You'll Understand	225
Sparrows and Blue Jays	226
I'm Sorry	227

Will I Ever be Good Enough?	228
In God's Eyes	229
An Explanation From The Heart	230
Soaring High Above the Clouds	231
Giving God My Heart	232
The Power of Words and Actions	233
By Your Side	234
The Tears That Come Down Like Rain	235
A List of Lessons	236
The Beauty of Time	237
As The Wind Blows	238
Writing Your Name In The Sand	239
Roses from The Heart	240
Spending Forever With You	241
I Love You	242
What Is True Love?	243
What Can Be Seen?	244
It's Time You Know My Battle Scars	245
The Fragile Heart	247
Stepping Into A Fairytale	248
A Table For Two	249
An Anchor of Love	250
The Forever Child	251
When the Time Comes	253

Part One

Letters to My Guardian Angel

Dear Guardian Angel,

I know you're at peace,
Being by God's side...
In the heavenly kingdom,
Watching over me.

I know that one day,
I'll see you again...
But it'll never be easy,
Living a life...
Where you're no longer here.

There's no phone to call,
Or a way to visit heaven...
And some nights,
Are so much harder than others...
To accept the fact,
That I have to wait till my time comes...
To have another one of your hugs,
Or a conversation with you.

I've asked God,
WHY?!?
More times that I can count...

And when I first lost you,
I even asked him to take me too...
For I didn't want to live without you,
But he eventually showed me why...
I needed to keep breathing,
And it's to keep your memory alive.

If I don't remember you,
Then who will?

If I don't keep your legacy alive,
Then who will make sure...
That your life's work lives on?

You have watched me grow,
As you helped God raise me...
And you continue to cheer me on,
But you're doing it from heaven now.

I've become stronger,
Since you first left earth...
But there are times where,
I'm weak and need you here...
Or a way to contact you,
And I try to pray more...
When that happens,
But sometimes it's difficult...
To find the words to pray,
Even though...
You probably know,
What I would say.

Even though I may not,
See the signs right away...
I know that you send them,
Down from heaven...
To help remind me,
That you'll always be...
Looking out for me.

I know that even though,
I may not be able to see you...
Or fully feel your presence,
You'll always be with me...
Until the end of time.

These letters I write,
Are poems for you...
Because you were,
My rock...
And the main one,
Who made the bad days...
Not seem as terrible.

My letters and poems,
Are also a way of healing...
Because sometimes,
It feels like you're still here…
When I pick up the pen and write,
So I'll continue,
To write these letters…
Until God calls me to my heavenly home.

You were my guardian on earth,
You were an important role...
Into making me into who I am today,
And now you're my guardian angel...
Who tries to never let me forget,
The worth that my earthly mark has...
Because you know that I have,
What it takes...
To make the world a better place.

The Final Hours

We never know,
When our final hours will occur.
The mark we make-
Will live on forever,
Through others.
When our final hours greet us,
We mustn't weep-
For we shall be glad,
For what we had.
Don't wait for tomorrow,
They may be our final hours.

When I'm Gone

Time on earth is limited,
Eventually time will be up.
When I'm gone,
Don't make this a goodbye-
When I go...
Think of it as,
I'll see you again someday.
It's normal to mourn,
But celebrate life.
Everyone leaves a mark,
On the world-
Even you.

The Key

My heart had a wall,
That guarded it-
You then tore it down.
My heart is a lock,
I gave you the key-
You used it to unlock my heart,
Then you hid it from further use.
My wall slowly going up again,
The lock slowly closing,
I love you-
Do you love me?

The Weeping Heart

The heart weeps,
When losing loved ones.
We must know,
That our loved ones aren't gone,
For they'll always be with us.
The weeping heart,
Is never alone-
No matter how empty it feels.
Weeping hearts-
Hope for tomorrow,
And live for today.

Tear Filled Raindrops

These raindrops that fall on treetops,
Are messages sent from above.

The Heavenly Father,
Walks with...
And guides His people.

The Lord's people are on Earth,
But they're also up in Heaven.

These raindrops that fall on treetops,
Are the same ones...

That fall on all rooftops,
And each acre of land.

The people on Earth shed tears,
And miss their loved ones...

That have traveled,
To their Heavenly home.

The people in Heaven,
Are Guardian Angels...

Of their loved ones on Earth,
But they too shed tears.

The raindrops that fall from the sky,
Are messages from above...

Because it's our loved ones,
In Heaven letting us know...

Through their tears,
That they miss being with us too.

Our guardian angels are safe,
And in a beautiful peaceful place...

But that doesn't mean,
That they'll forget to watch over...

Those they left behind but will forever love,
So they'll send those they love...

Reminders that say,
We'll continue to be in their hearts as well.

The raindrops we see,
Will always be tear filled...

So let's listen closely and let,
Our guardian angels legacy live on.

Hero

Who is your hero?
NOT all heroes,
Have or wear capes.
Some heroes,
Blend in with you and I-
Through appearance.
The hero part of someone,
Comes from within.
Listen to your heart,
It will lead you home.

Messages from the Sky

The stars whisper,
The stories of the past...
Reminding me not to take,
This life for granted.

Everything could be over,
In the blink of an eye...

And people may not get,
The chance to say goodbye.

If you love someone,

Remind them...

If you care about someone,

Then make it known...

The stars may whisper,
But there are things...
That everyone shouldn't,
Stay quiet about.

As the stars continue,
To twinkle and whisper...
Giving me hope for tomorrow,
The moon begins to glimmer...
And she calls out to you and I,
Saying rest child,
You've had a busy day.

The moon teaches us that it's okay,
To unwind and relax our mind...
Because life can be hectic,
And she doesn't want us...
To be overwhelmed and stressed.

As I get ready for bed,

I feel God hugging me...

Reminding me that he's,

Always protecting me...

Even when I'm sleeping.

I'm God's Child,
And so are you...
So as you fall asleep tonight,
Remember...
That you are loved,
By your Heavenly Father...
And that you,
Are NOT a mistake...
Your life has purpose,
Even if it's hard to see at times.

Once we're fast asleep,
The moon says goodnight...
To each of the stars,
For she knows...
Our guardian angels,
Shine brightest through them.

When the sun comes out,
The stars and the moon...

Hand her the spotlight,

For they know...
That without her,
The world wouldn't be the same.

When the sun comes out,
She's wakes up the people...
For it's a new day,
That the Lord made...
Specifically for,
His children.

The sun shines,
Giving us the okay...
To rise and shine,
But she reminds us...
To be thankful for life,
For we don't know...
How much time,
We have left here.

When the sun goes down,
The stars and the moon...
Come back out,
For the nightly routine...
That God has given us,
To comfort our hearts.

The Spooked Horse

My brain goes,
A thousand miles-
Like a spooked horse.
A million thoughts,
Run through my mind-
Like a spooked horse,
On a racetrack.
Life is like the sky-
With light and darkness.
Don't stay spooked,
Everything's okay-
In the end.

Hidden

A smile is a mask,
That hides the pain-
Fooling others,
Into thinking someone's happy.
The eyes of a person,
Shows their pain and storm.
The eyes remove,
The smiles mask.
Heartache is shown,
In more ways than one-
Just pay attention,
You'll finally see.

The Quiet Poet

My poetry is the only place,
Where people I'm not close with...
Ever get to see my heart,
Anywhere near my sleeve.

My poetry is my safe place,
The place where I know...
I can fall apart,
Or smile for a while.

My poetry has a part of me,
That only the pen and paper see...
For they've been with me,
Through all of life's battles.

I'm the quiet poet,
For my outside voice...
May be pretty quiet,
But my writing voice is loud...
Because I refuse to silence,
The poet within me.

Each day I write what's inside my heart,
And some days it's more than others...
But something the Lord says,
Each time that I pick up my pen...
Is that in the end I'll be okay,
For he'll never let go of my hand.

The soul is the harmony that goes along to the heart's song.

Shine

My heart is a flame,
Trying to stay lit underwater.
Breath by breath,
Make the most of life-
No matter the obstacle.
Life is a precious miracle,
Never settle for less.
Do not fear,
Your flame will shine bright-
Even under the waters,
My hand is yours.

A Life Brand New

I had forgotten what it was like,
To truly smile.
My genuine smile faded,
When I started sinking.

Don't tell me you're sorry for something,
If you plan on doing it again.
Don't tell me you love me,
If your actions are going to prove otherwise.

I gave you the key to my heart,
I had given you my all...
I let you tear down my walls,
Giving me a life brand new.

I had forgotten what it was like,
To truly smile.
My genuine smile faded,
When I started sinking.

A hand was held out to me,
Knowing I had forgotten how to swim.
That same hand is held out to you,
Will you take it?

Everyone has storms in life-
For the storms make us cherish,
The good times more than before.

The world is full of hatred,
But it's also full of love.
On this journey called life-
Know you're not alone,
And you're always loved.

Suffering in Silence

Wondering what I deserve-
Crying alone at night,
Whispering I'm worthless.
Words have hurt me,
Hands have hurt me,
Now I can't look in a mirror-
Without regret.
I'm broken.
If I deserved better,
I would of been given a sign.
Crying alone at night,
Just wanting,
To be worth it.
I'm silently calling out for help-
Look into my eyes,
Instead of at my smile.

Writing Everything Down

When I pick up the pen it's like,
A whole new world begins...
And when the pen meets the paper,
That's when all of me is seen...

My past,

My present...

AND,

My Future.

Everything that I've been,
Along with everything I am...
And everything that I will be,
All end up making grand entrances...
Into this world because,
I can't hide forever.

As time goes on my heart will eventually,
Write everything down to give everyone...
A part of me to carry with them,
Wherever they may go.

The Angel's Lesson

You killed a part of the angel,

That's inside of me...

And you made me want,

To crawl into a ball and die.

You filled my head with doubts,

You lowered my self esteem...

And you tried to feed me to the wolves,

For you only cared about one thing...

Yourself.

You hurt me,

In more ways than one...

Inside and out,

And you left me with scars.

Seeing the red flags,

Seeing the warning signs...

Should be easy to point out.

Being used to the pain,

Made all the alerts...

That would tell me to leave,

Arrive way later,

Than they should have.

I thought I knew,

What true love was...

But I didn't feel worthy,

Of a love so raw and real...

One like my grandparents,

Until God made me...

See that I deserve,

Way better than you.

After you,

It took me a while...

To heal from all the damage,

And there's still a few scars...

But they don't define me,

And I won't let them try to.

I'll never see you again,

So thank you for...

All of the hard lessons,

That you taught me.

It took some time,

But I found my one true love...

Because God blessed me with him,

When I was truly ready...

For a magical love story,

That has no end.

Now the part of the angel within me,

That you thought you had killed...

Has blossomed and spread her wings,

For she finally learned how to fly.

This Is Your Sign

When was the last time,
You woke up with a smile?
When was the last time,
It felt good to be alive?

When did you start,
Hating life?
Will you ever feel worthy,
Of the love you deserve?

If you're looking for a sign,
That everything will be alright...
This is it.
If you're looking for a sign,
That life will get better in time...
This is it.
If you're looking for a sign,
Asking you to stay here with me...
Instead of running away and dying,
This is it.

All of your worry tears shed,
Along with the feeling of defeat...
Eventually lead to a happy ending,
And you may not believe me right now...
When I remind you that you're important,
And that's okay for a little while...
Because life wasn't made to be easy,
So remember to look at the stars...
When life seems too hard,
For you to carry on.

Forever Holding Hands

The pain I've gone through,
Has been on an endless loop...
At least until I found you,
In God's timing.

I still have battle scars,
But they're all worth it...
Because the broken road,
Has lead me to you.

Your touch is healing,
To my heart and soul...
Your touch is healing,
To my mind...
In your arms is where I belong,
So thank you for loving me...
For the person God created me to be.

You're my home and my safe place,
So thank you for holding my hand...
Through the rough moments,
And through the beautiful times...
Of this thing called life.

I'm truly blessed,
To have you by my side...
Forever and always.

I love more than you'll ever know,
But I hope that you know...
I treasure every second with you,
And that I always will.

Giving It All To God

I look up to the stars,
As much as I can...
For they help remind me,
That my guardian angels...
Aren't super far away,
And that they'll forever be...
Right by my side,
Even if at times I feel alone.

There are times where the weight,

That the world puts on my shoulders...

Becomes too heavy for me to carry.

Some things are harder,
To completely give to God...
But I must trust him,
And give him everything...
That rests or stirs in my heart,
For his love is everlasting...
And he only wants what's best,
For his beloved children.

It's okay to ask God,
The hard questions...
WHY?
Being a common one.

It's okay to cry,
The Lord reminds his people...
That they don't always,
Have to be strong...
Because God,
Is always with them...
Helping everyone,
Through the storms of life.

Whether you feel,

Alone or not…

Look to the Lord.

God will light the way...
And fill your heart with peace,
Giving it a home...
With your Heavenly Father,
Who will never abandon you.

Day and Night

The sun is bright and beautiful.
The daylight warms the heart.
The night sky is dark.
Look to the sky-
For you will find,
Stars light up the night.
When going through pain,
Know it won't be dark forever.
Let your starlight shine-
Make your mark.

Finally Home

Looking for a map,
A way to finally be home.
Melancholy feelings,
Try and trap me-
But hope swoops in,
To keep me going.
A hand is stretched out,
To save me-
I'm finally home,
With God by my side.
Finally at home,
I have found peace.

Imperfection

I make mistakes,
But I learn.
Life has wondrous gifts,
But it has obstacles.
Looks fade,
While personality remains.
You see imperfection-
But I am who I am.
Everyone and everything,
Has imperfections.
See beyond,
My imperfection-
Accept me for me.

Blood

My heart is pumping the blood,
That runs through my veins.
My heart leads me home,
My brain following-
Sending it vital signals.
My heart pumps blood,
That runs in my veins.
At any moment,
My heart may stop.
Tomorrow might not come,
At least we have today.

Fish Out of Water

Like fish swim in the sea,
We walk on land-
Never knowing,
When our last breath will occur.
Take today for granted-
Become a fish out of water.
We may swim with the fish,
But fish won't walk with us.
Value each moment-
Make today count.

Am I

The feeling of emptiness,
Leads us-
Down a dark winding road.
Am I wanted,
Dead or alive?
The feeling of hope,
Leads us-
Down a starlit path.
Am I wanted,
Dead or alive?
Make the most
Out of your day-
Don't wait for tomorrow,
Start your journey today.

Finding Peace on the Mountain

The fog watches me sob,
From time to time...
So the wind takes a look,
At the trouble...
That's found,
Within my soul...
And it finds questions,
I usually keep to myself.

Am I good enough?

Will I ever be brave enough?

Will I ever have the courage,
To stand up and say...
Today is my day?

What will it take,
To regain my voice...
For I just want to rejoice!
The devil is trying,
To keep my praise on mute...
But Lord please do NOT,
Let him succeed...
Because Father,
I only want you.

Lord you're my healer and Shepard,
Please help me through this storm...
For on my own I'm overwhelmed,
But in you I find peace.

So Father God I pray,
That you help make...
Your presence known,
To all who are weary...
Including me,
For you are bigger...
Than any mountain,
That may come our way.

The Waltz

Looking at the world,
While thinking of the universe-
We dance alone to a tune.
The heart aches,
For someone to waltz in-
Joining our dance.
The sun along with the stars,
All watch the lonesome dance-
Your hand being taken,
When the time is right.

God's Blessings

As the rain hits the roof,
My tears fill the room...
Creating pitter patter sounds,
That echo all around.

As God tries,

To remove my doubts...

As God tries,

To calm my fears...

And as God tries,

To remove my melancholy feelings...

He reminds me,
To count my blessings...
Instead of worrying so much,
For he needs me...
To understand that Through Christ,
ALL THINGS ARE POSSIBLE!

TRUE LOVE NEVER DISAPPEARS

Each sunset,
Reminds me...
Of the day we met.

Each sunrise,
Reminds me...
Of the love in your eyes.

I've been hurt,
AND...
I've been broken,
BUT...
God lead my heart,
To where I needed to be.

Every fear and tear,
Tries to disappear...
When you're near,
Because...
Every hope and smile,
Comes alive when you're here.

Not knowing the Lord's plan,
But trusting it anyway...
Has given us true love,
And a forever home...
In each other's hearts,
Because when love is real...
It won't ever disappear,
No matter what happens.

As you hold my hand,
We prepare for the future...
While living in the now,
For with each breath I take...
I renew my vow to you,
And I'm so glad...
That God gave me you,
To spend forever and always with.

The Small Puppet

Showing the world the colors,
That lay within your soul...
Doesn't mean that you need,
To change your identity.

Showing the world,
Each color of your heart...
Means staying true to yourself,
Instead of becoming...
The puppet with a small voice,
That others may want you to be.

You are powerful.
You are important.
You are special.

God gave you this life,
So even when you get knocked down...
And feel like you can't go on,
Or you feel your faith shake...
Remember to reach out your hand...
And accept the love of Christ,
Because through him...
You'll be able to stand again,
And the strength you once had will return.

In life people don't get rough drafts,
Because life is meant to be lived...
As if tomorrow may never come,
And if tomorrow does come,
Yesterday can be used as a guide...
For you to reflect upon,
To help you make the most out of today.

Use what the Lord gave you,
And let your light shine...
Show the world the colors,
That have painted your heart and soul...
For even if your life's painting,
Isn't close to being finished...
It may just inspire someone.

Showing your colors,
That come from within your heart and soul...
May give someone the bravery or courage,
To be who they truly wish to be.

When you stay true to yourself,
Instead of being who the world decides...
You may do more than just inspire someone,
Because you may end up saving a life or two...
Because when people feel like puppets,
They may feel like giving up.

When someone shows another person,
That it's okay to be themselves...
It'll reveal to them that they don't,
Have to hide their identity...
Even when the world tries,
To make them feel as small as a puppet.

Words vs. Actions

You say that you care,

But it feels like...

You're just bending my ear.

Are you being real,

OR are you just telling me...

What I wanna hear?

Your words become silent,

When your actions don't match up...

So let your actions be the echo,

That lets your voice be heard.

Honesty

If you can't be honest with me,
Then you may as well flee.
Save us both time-
By being genuine,
From the beginning.
If you can't be honest with me,
Then please just let me be.

Air

When life gets difficult-
It feels like we hold our breath.
Being human,
Doesn't allow us,
To hold our breath for long.
We need air.
Eventually we have to,
Catch a breath,
To fill our lungs with air.
We can either swim or sink-
What will you do?

Motivation

It's time to wake up,
What's your motivation?
Don't let others,
Control you thoughts-
Keeping you from who you are.
Have motivation,
To chase your dreams.
Sitting still,
Dreams stay dreams...
Unless you put in the effort.
What's motivating you today?

The Song of Life

My heart keeps a beat,
While my soul is its harmony.
My heart seems to be,
The punching bag people use...
My heart has been,
In an immense amount of pain.
Maybe one day-
Things will be okay again.
With God,
I can get through anything.
Life is a song,
With low notes and high notes...
My heart keeps a beat,
While my soul is its harmony.

Footprints

The clock is always ticking-
The amount of time,
We have on earth is unknown.
From each breath we take,
We leave a footprint or mark-
On people's hearts.
Even after we pass,
Footprints can not be erased.
We never truly die,
For our spirit lives on.

The House of Tears

I have to hide from the cold outside,

For I can't always be fine...

So I sit here looking for an outlet,

Or someplace safe to cry...

While I watch time pass me by,

Praying for a miracle to arrive.

The devil has tried countless times,

To drown me and freeze my heart...

But God Is by my side through thick and thin,

So no matter how many times...

The enemy may attempt to harm me,

I know that I'll be safe...

In the hills and mountains,

Along with the Valleys of life...

Because Jesus will forever,

Be looking out for me.

As I cry these tears of fear,

My Heavenly Father...

Holds me near,

Reminding me...

That everything will be okay,

Even when the future isn't always clear.

My house of tears is fairly private,

Because I will never...

Wear my heart on my sleeve,

For I need to take care of my heart...

During each storm that's thrown my way,

Instead of giving the devil power...

To possibly destroy me,

Because I know that the Lord...

Has so much in store for me,

And I don't want to throw it all away.

The Last Petal

I'm a growing flower-
Eventually,
I'll lose all my petals.
I blossom in spring and summer,
I face hardships-
Like fall and winter.
My last petal of the year,
Will one day fall.
When one season ends-
A new one begins,
To make life everlasting.

Vision

The vision of love,
The vision of care,
The vision of hope-
All come from within.
Miracles can happen,
Every now and then-
Make the most out of your time.
The vision of today,
Prepares us for tomorrow.
Even in the dark-
Let your visions shine bright.

Reminders

Everywhere I go,
I see reminders of you.
The reminders show me,
You're still here.
Melancholy feelings,
Sometimes take over.
You want me to be happy,
Trust me-
I'm trying to be.
Reminders comfort me,
For you'll always be with me...
You made your mark.

Blessings In Disguise

The crickets call to remind me,
That pain is temporary...
And to tell me,
That it's okay to fall apart.

The caterpillar gives me hints,
That everything is going to be okay...
Even when change is on the way.
When the transformation,
Turns the caterpillar into a butterfly...
It reminds me that my history,
Can be a blessing in disguise for my future.

The seeds are planted,
From all of life's beauty...
Requiring care and prayer,
Along with time to grow...
Because some things,
Don't happen overnight.
As the flowers begin to bloom,
They remove any gloom...
That may have arrived,
When the storms came...
And tried to destroy me,
Along with my hopes and dreams.

The sun rises,
And the sun sets...
But I need to keep in mind,
That with God's help...
Anything is possible,
Even when life is hard to understand.

There are signs everywhere,
Asking me to hold on...
Because nature knows,
That my time here on earth...
Is far from done...
And that IF I gave up,
It would hurt...
Those around me,
While breaking God's heart.

These signs that surround me,
Show me that miracles...
Happen when least expected,
Because God is a way maker...
For he loves his children,
More than they'll ever know.

Don't say you "love" someone unless it's honest & true... AND if it's true, then you'll also end up showing it to them through all that you do.

***Do not try to force someone to love you,
let them love you naturally.
It's in the difficult times mixed with the happy
times that reveal who loves you for you.***

One More Chance

Some people give out,
Chance after chance-
Over and over again,
Don't waste these chances.
Everyone has a breaking point...
Once someone walks away-
Saying that they're done,
They'll be gone for good.
Treasure what you have,
While you have it.

Trust

Trust is fragile,
It can be broken-
All at once or little by little.
You can try to fix it-
Knowing it'll never be the same,
The damage was made.
Trust isn't given freely,
For it is earned.
If you love someone,
Show them that you do-
Before it's to late.

Wings

The heart is a butterfly,
That flaps its wings-
In the sky.
Before the butterfly,
Can take flight,
It must start out-
As a caterpillar,
That learns to walk.
The little things add up,
Making them mean the most.
After you walk,
It'll be time to fly.

Heaven's Door

Loved ones have walked,
Through heaven's door.
Until we meet again-
In heaven,
It's farewell.
One day,
It'll be our time-
To walk through heaven's door.
We mustn't forget,
That the mark we've made-
Forever lives on,
Like a stain that won't come out.

The Shield of Protection

Satan has tried,
To kill me before...
BUT,
He's been unsuccessful...
And I'll never let him win,
For he can't outsmart the Lord.

I have been hurt before,
In more ways than one...
But God came and rescued me,
Reminding me that he has my back.

I have my Fathers love,
Which is a shield...
That protects me,
From the enemy's crimes.

When Satan tries to attack,
He has to go through the Lord...
To get to me,
Because I'm not...
Going to give power,
To the one that will try to destroy me.

God is more,
Than "good"...
For he is wonderful.

God's love is everlasting,
And he never lets...
His children drown,
For he's always with them.

If you don't believe,
The same things as me...
That's okay,
I won't force you to.

I worship and love Jesus,
The one who died...
On the cross for you and me,
Because he loves us...
More than,
We'll ever know.

Thank you Father,
For always being...
There for me,
Even though...
There were times,
My faith gently shook.

Father help me continue,
To trust you...
Even in life's storms,
For your love is all I need.

Roots, Branches, and Leaves

These roots,
Keep this tree of life standing.
Have few people,
Become your roots-
So you stay grounded.
The branches provide nutrients,
But they may break-
Like some people support you,
Without being the safety net.
These leaves you see...
Or temporary people,
Provide light and guidance
While eventually drifting away.
Life may be painful sometimes-
For it just allows you to grow...
Your life is precious,
The world needs you-
Just like the world needs,
This tree of life.

Masquerade

The melancholy feeling,
Masked by the simplest of smiles-
At this masquerade.
You never know...
Who's smile is true or forbidden.
Look at the masked face,
And look into the eyes of eternity.
Through the eyes,
You'll travel to the heart and soul.
There are no maps,
To guide you on this journey...
You have to trust your instincts.
A smile can be dangerous,
While being beautiful and inviting.
The mind, heart, and soul...
Know where you need to go and when.
You must not be late for each masquerade-
For you have the potential that's needed,
To save the day.

The Sorrow In My Heart

My melancholy joy,
Is a song for the Lord...
That's found in my heart,
Since when my soul is aching...
Jesus restores any hope,
That may have been lost in the storm.

Grace is found,
In Christ the Lord...
Who allows me to swim,
Instead of drowning.

When melancholy feelings,
Put weight on my shoulders...
Joy finds a way,
 To lift any sorrow from within.

My melancholy joy,
Is found in the hands...
Of my father,
That gave me life...
For he knows his children,
Are stronger than they think.

The Listening Heart

As we have slept underneath,
The very same sky...
I had a dream of peace,
And then God took you and I...
Brought us together,
And turned us into one.

So as he listens to my heart,
I hope he knows...
That the reason why,
My heart still quietly beats...
Is because of him,
For he rescued me.

As he listens to my heart,
I hope he knows...
That there's no place better,
Than right by his side.

But most of all,
As he listens to my heart...
I hope that he knows,
I love him more than he'll ever know.

A Voice In The Wind

I hear your voice,

Eco in the soft wind...

Telling me that,

It's okay to forgive myself.

You tell me that,
You're safe now...
And that it's okay,
To loosen my grip.

You encourage me,
To let go a little more of you...
For you hate that I'm still,
Hurting this bad after your passing.

I'll always wish that you were,

Still here with me...

For I miss,

Having you near.

But the wind continues,
To carry your voice...
Directly placing it,
In my ear...
And sending it,
To my heart.
Through the Lord's will,
I've made it this far...
Yes I've had ups and downs,
But the memory of you...
Will always be safe and sound,
In my heart, soul, and mind...
And I'll continue doing what I can,
To keep your legacy alive.

I loved you then,
And I love you now...
Even though you're in heaven,
And I'm still on earth.

I don't know when or if I'll ever,

Fully be okay after losing you...

But one thing I'm sure of,

Is that I'll always treasure...

The years where you were,

Right beside me...

Making memories,

That would never die.

Holding On

I'm holding on-
To each day alive, & to my hope.
I need to hold on,
To what matters most.
Life is taken away,
So quickly.
When I breath my final breath-
Will you be satisfied,
With how everything ended?
Make each breath count,
Before it's to late.

They Told Me So

I gave my whole heart to you-
Piece by piece,
I'm being broken again.
I'm the one that's forgettable-
They tell me I'm loved,
Am I really?
Tell me this,
Why I am replaced so quickly?

They weren't right for you-
You're giving them,
To much credit.
You are loved-
Don't let the toxic ones,
Tell you different.

Living Life in the Blues

No one promised,
Life would be easy.

Live today,
Like tomorrow doesn't exist...
For it may never come.

Find happiness,
Amongst life's blues.

Your smile could heal,
Someone's nightmare.

Life may not be easy,
But your life matters.

The Call of Tears

The life we were living,
Was to the fullest...
Or so I thought.

The phone rang.
When I saw it was you calling,
I answered in a heartbeat.

It wasn't you,
That spoke when I picked up...
I realized then,
This would be a call of tears.
The voice then told me,
That you passed away.

My heart shattered...
As tears rolled down my face.
This wasn't just a call,
It was the call of tears.

Why did our time,
Have to end so soon?
I wasn't ready...
For the call of tears.
Life will never be the same,
Now that you're in heaven.

Your mark on the world won't disappear.

The call of tears,
Makes you appreciate the little things...
More than before.

The Missing Piece of My Heart

I never knew how much time,
I'd get to have with you...
But I didn't imagine,
That you'd leave so soon.

God called you,
To your heavenly home...
And when he did,
I felt all alone.
My heart and soul,
Along with my mind...
Couldn't grasp the reality,
That you were gone.

I couldn't hear your voice,
And I couldn't see you...
Which left me scared,
To live a life without you.
I'm trying to be strong,
I'm trying to hold on...
But without you by my side,
It's hard to keep living.

I'm trying to forgive myself,
For wanting to join you...
When you joined Jesus in heaven,
But it's so hard.
Everyday seems to be,
A trip down memory lane...
Because so much,
Reminds me of you.

You were,
You are...
And will always be,
My hero.
No matter how much,
Time passes...
I'll always miss you,
And wish you were here.

I've begged on my knees,
Asking God why I didn't...
Get to say goodbye,
But for a while I had no answer.

As the days pass by,
I have to remind myself...
That I'll see you again,
Someday when my time comes...
But in the meantime,
I know you'll always be near...
Even though my time on earth,
Isn't over yet.

Sometimes I'm able,
To get through the day...
Without breaking down,
But until I see you again...
A piece of my heart,
Will always be missing...
Even though I know,
That you'll always be with me.

The Different Levels of Pain

Everyone experiences,
Pain differently...
For it comes in levels.
Physical pain-
Is the most obvious,
For it's easier to spot.
Emotional pain-
Is more discrete...
For it's less noticeable,
Unless you go beyond what's revealed.

With emotional pain,
We may notice the small signs others give-
But there are greater levels,
Than what meets the eye...
The loss of a loved one,
Or a breakup perhaps.
Maybe things aren't okay at home-
Maybe you got bad news...
The list goes on and on.
With emotional pain,
We may notice signs given to us-
But there are greater levels,
Than what meets the eye...

Pain comes in different levels.
We must train our eyes...
To look beyond,
The mask some people use-
For it may save a life.
You may be someone's lifeline,
Without even realizing it.

God Called Me Home

My time has come,
To leave the earth.
I've lived the life,
I was supposed to live.

The mark I left on the world,
Will hopefully last forever...
If you eventually forget me,
I'll understand.
My time on earth was limited.
I'm thankful,
For the good and the bad memories.
I'll miss my earth life dearly,
But God called me home.

I'll forever watch over you,
Along with the others I loved.
I may not be there on earth,
But I'm not far away...
For I'll always be in your heart.

If you cry when remembering me,
Know that each breath you take...
Is allowing the impact I had on you,
To live on —
I'll never truly be gone.

I may not be there on earth,
But I'm not far away...
For I'll always be in your heart.

World Peace

Every holiday season,
There's laughter and cheer...

And we're told there will be,
Peace on Earth...

But will it be here by midnight?

There's peace within my soul,
Because of the Lord my Father...

But the world is troubled,
For not everyone trusts him.

World peace can start,
With you and me...

As we keep guardian angels,
In our hearts forever...

But as we do this,
It is important that we...

Play our part and make our mark,
For we all have a purpose here on Earth.

Empty Promises

You make empty promises...
Your next move being a mystery.

Try being honest for once...
Only make promises you'll keep.

Your empty promises,
Make me wonder...
When they'll be real.

Honesty will save us time,
And it'll try to save our hope.

The Lost Heartbeat

Side by side,
Facing life together...
For all eternity.

You got sick one day...

After you got sick,
Each day became a harder battle.
We had hope that tomorrow…....
Would take its time to get here,
So that today could last a little longer.
Each passing day,
Was a battle...
That couldn't necessarily be won.

Memories were created with you,
That will never fade or be erased.

You lost your battle,
Your heartbeat eventually stopped.
Making me lose my breath.
The room grew eerily quiet...
I knew the day would come,
But I most definitely wasn't ready.
I wanted to go with you,
But my time wasn't up yet-
God wanted me to keep your legacy alive...
For our bond could never be broken.
You're an angel in heaven,
Guiding me through each tomorrow.

Goodbye Darkness

The sun shines,
As the caterpillar...
Gains its wings,
And learns to fly.

Rainy days may come,
But with each raindrop...
Or tear that falls,
There's always a star...
Shining brightly,
To stop complete darkness...
From finding a way,
To erase each hopeful heart.

The lord shines,
His love and light...
Upon our love story,
Turning us into one.

Through the highs,
And the lows...

Through the ups,
And the downs...

In sickness,
And in health...

For no matter what happens,
It'll forever be us...
Against the world,
With God leading us.

The Golden Heart

Once a heart of gold,
Gets hurt numerous times...
It will freeze-
Ice taking over.
A kind and warm hearted soul,
Will unfreeze this frozen heart...
Slowly but surely.
Unfreezing a heart of gold,
Takes time and patience.
Once the heart is unfrozen,
Its cracks are revealed.
The heart may not be fully fixed,
But there's a healthy repair.

Life is like swimming.
There's shallow water...
Where it's easy to swim or even float.
Then there's the deep water,
If you're there to long...
It could attempt to take you under.
If you have a heart of gold,
You must be careful.
If you let it freeze because of the pain...
Don't lose hope,
A kind and warm hearted soul is never far behind.

Time will always pass,
So make sure it's spent wisely.
The golden hearts,
May physically part from the world,
But the legacy left behind...
Isn't able to be erased.

A Stained Glass Window

My eyes are a stained glass window,
To those who take the time...
To look into the heart and soul.
My story is more than what you see.

The stained glass window,
Glistens in the sun and rain.
You may not see the storm...
But if you look hard enough,
You'll find my story.
The smiles I've seen have created,
A ray of light so bright it shines.
The tears my eyes have seen,
But also created...
Is the rain that comes-
Every so often.

Most people don't think twice,
To see if someone is genuinely okay.
The stained glass window,
Is a combination-
Of joy and melancholy.
A smile may be broken...
So look into someone's eyes,
At their stained glass window eyes.
Take time to appreciate everything in life,
Before it's too late.

My eyes are a stained glass window,
To those who take the time...
To look into the heart and soul.

Suicidal Thoughts

Wanting the pain to end,
Drowning in everything going on...
Suicidal thoughts making an appearance.
Why does this have to happen to me?
Life is too unfair...

Trying to push the suicidal thoughts away,
I wonder would anyone notice if I was gone?
I wonder if my life actually makes,
That big of an impact on the world?

Someone's been holding their hand out for me,
I just got so lost that I ignored it at first.

If you're feeling hopeless,
If you feel suicidal,
If you feel like giving up...
Try to open your stained glass window eyes,
A hand is stretched out for you too.
Even though giving up may be tempting,
Keep holding on.
Your life matters more than you know.
Your stained glass window eyes,
May be the very thing that saves someone...
You could be someone's hero and lifeline.
It's okay if you need to ask for help,
In fact it's encouraged to ask for help.
Even if you disagree with me,
Your life is precious.

Moment by Moment

I came into this world,
Not knowing how it all works.

Through the wonderful moments,
And through the tough moments...
I've grown stronger than imagined.
Everything that has happened,
Has shaped me into the person I am.
I may not be,
The toughest person around-
But I stay true to who I am.

I came into this world,
Not knowing how it all works.
With each day,
I learn something new...
For life is a test.
The test of life is a series,
Of doors and windows...
Known as opportunities and chances.

I am who I am,
You are who you are.
We live today,
Like tomorrow doesn't exist.
I came into this world,
Not knowing how it all works.
Moment by moment,
Memories are being created...
To last a lifetime.

A Christmas Eve Prayer

It's Christmas Eve,

So before I go to sleep…

I close my eyes,

And take a breath in and out.

After I take a deep breath,
I fold my hands and begin…
Saying a prayer because,
Even though you've been gone…
For several years now,
The sting is still here.

Christmas isn't the same,
Without your laughter…
Or without your cheer,
BUT most of all…
Christmas isn't the same,
Without you here.

In my Christmas Eve prayer,

I ask the Lord to give me strength…

For Christmas Day and I ask him,

To give me strength for all the days…

That lay ahead since my journey's not done yet.

In my Christmas Eve prayer,
I ask the Lord…

To deliver a message,
From me to you…

For I need you to know,
That I love and miss you.

My Christmas Eve prayers,
Always lead me down...
Memory lane for a visit,
And in a way memory lane...
Allows me to remain hopeful,
For it tells me that...
I may not see you,
But you'll never leave me.

If you were here on Earth,

Celebrating Jesus with us…

I wonder what you'd tell me,

For you always gave great advice.

If you were here on Earth,

I'd give you a hug one more time…

And I'd thank you for everything,

Since I never said it enough.

You're celebrating Christmas,
In heaven with Jesus...
And I'm sure that's beautiful,
I just hope that you've had...
Another wonderful year,
In your heavenly home.

As another year goes by,
Where only the memory of you...
Is able to make it feel like you're still near,
I hope that you know that life will never...
Be the same without you here,
Because you'll always be irreplaceable.

God since you hear my heart,

Please know that...

My guardian angel,

Will never be forgotten...

And I promise the mark,

That was left behind...

Will forever live on,

No matter how many years go by.

The Lord and The Lighthouse

When my heart, soul, and mind combine,
The organ music starts to play.
The bells and uplifting words,
Help destroy...
Anything the devil may throw my way.

The lighthouse starts to appear again,
For the lord's light...
Shines so very bright.
The lighthouse won't disappear,
But sometimes we lose sight of it...
When we listen to the world's chatter.
When my heart, soul, and mind combine,
The organ music starts to play.

When people meet me,
Do they feel that the lord is with them?
Do the people feel peace and love?
When my heart, soul, and mind combine,
The organ music starts to play.

The devil may have power,
But the lord's power is forever greater.
No matter what you believe,
Know that your life matters...
There's a shooting star in the sky,
That will always light up the night.
When my heart, soul, and mind combine,
The organ music starts to play.

The Porch Swing

Out on the porch swing,
It's just you and me...
Listening to the crickets sing.

After our late night snack,
We bow our heads...
And pray our evening prayer.

If one things for certain,
It's that true love is...
As delicate as a flower,
And it's more powerful...
Than most could imagine.

The porch swing of ours,
Sways back and fourth...
Full of so many memories,
Telling others...
About our forever love story.

You and I became one,
And God's plan was bigger...
Than we ever dreamed,
And he blessed us beyond belief.

We've listened to the crickets song,
Day after day for many years...
And it always reminded us,
That one day our time on Earth...
Would completely be done,
And he made sure we knew...
To make the most of our time.

A Winter Wonderland Holiday

The snow falls quietly in the night,

Taking away the fall leaves…

While looking for,

Things to be made right.

The next night there are,

Snowballs on the loose…

Looking for me and you,

So there's not much…

That we can do except join,

The winter wonderland.

Dancing and singing,

Laughing and smiling…

The holiday cheer comes out,

Replacing our fears.

The kiss of our snow angels,

Decorate the town…

Letting people know,

It's okay to let their guard down.

Now we head home,

To the place...

Where we'll be,

Safe and sound...

All through the night,

Under the Lords star.

I want you to know,

That I love all of you...

Including your battle scars,

So take my hand tonight...

Let's sit by the living room fire,

Looking at our Christmas tree lights...

And make one more memory,

Before we say goodnight.

The Two Become One

You claimed you loved me.
If what you said was true,
Your actions would have added up.
The way you treated me,
Never matched up with your words.

What if you never had,
All those words you said?
What if I never heard,
Your hypnotic and persuading voice?
Your actions are the echo to your words.
You claimed you loved me.

You've fooled me,
But I eventually caught on...
In the end your actions,
Told me what I really needed to know.
How you acted,
Revealed that your love is a lie.
You claimed you loved me.

A heart can only take so much abuse,
Before it gives up.
Hearts are fragile during heartbreak,
Allowing them to gain the strength they need.

Maybe one day,
You'll genuinely love someone.
When you love with your heart, soul, and mind...
Your words combine with your actions,
Letting the person you love,
Know that it's real.

My Love For Jesus

From a distance,
You can't hear...
My heartbeat,
For its lullaby...
Is fairly quiet,
And relaxed.

If you truly care,
Then when you look...
Into these eyes of mine,
You'll see my soul...
And eventually hear,
This quiet heartbeat...
That's protected by the Lord.

My heart isn't,
Displayed on my sleeve...
Because I take safety precautions,
Since not everyone...
Has pure intentions,
But my love for Jesus...
Will always show,
Even to those I hardly know.

The Stars In His Eyes

His eyes are like the stars,
For they hide so much pain...
Within their beauty.

As I hold him close,
And comfort him...
God whispers,
Everything will be okay.

Through all of life's,
Melancholy moments...
And joyful memories,
The vows we made...
Will forever live on.

In the world there are,
More love stories...
Than I can count,
But the story of us...
Will never have an ending,
Since true love never dies.

The World is Our Home

You pick on others,
Because they're different.

You try to dim someone's light,
So yours shines brighter.

The world doesn't revolve,
Around only one person.

The world revolves,
Around you and I...
Along with everyone else.

It's never okay to be a bully.

How would you feel,
If someone treated you..
The way you treat others?

You pick on others,
Because they're different.
If we were all the same,
Life may not be as interesting.

Let's make the world,
Feel more like home...
And be more accepting of others.
Our mark on the world will last a lifetime,
While each act of kindness never fades.

The Unseen Future

You're unpredictable,
Like a book or a movie...
That keeps me,
On the edge of my seat.
I never know,
What to expect...
So each day is an adventure.

On good days and bad days,
There's always something to learn.

If I say I love you,
It's because I mean it...
If you took those words away,
I hope my actions reveal my love.

I never know,
What to expect...
So each day is an adventure.
Change is inevitable,
So if you grow tired of me,
Know you'll always...
Have a place in my heart.
If you decided to say goodbye,
Please do it quick...
Goodbyes are forever.
I'm much better at farewell,
For I know I'll see that person...
Again someday.

Creating Connections Through Questions

When surrounded by rhetorical questions,
Metaphors become more frequently used...
Because it's known that one voice,
Can influence others.

Metaphors tend to help people see,
Hypothetical situations...
Encouraging them to ask,
Questions such as...

What if?

Or,

Why?

These questions help people see,
Each new day clearly...
And they show the world,
Not to settle for less...
Because bigger pictures,
Are painted when people...
Broaden their horizons,
And follow their heart.

Metaphors give people,

A way to be truly heard...

Because each metaphor,

Can make someone ponder or think...

About what's being said,

And that creates a connection.

Connections are important,
Because after all...
Everyone leaves a mark,
Or a footprint here on earth...
And in the hearts,
Of the people around them.

So if you have a question,
Don't hesitate to ask it...
If you have something to say,
Don't be afraid to speak...
And if you have a dream,
Don't be afraid to chase it.

Wandering Thoughts

Underneath the starlit sky,
My thoughts begin to wander.
What kind of life am I living?
Am I making the mark on the world,
That I want to make?
Would people notice...
If I wasn't here anymore?

Underneath the starlit sky,
My thoughts begin to wander.
There's daytime and nighttime,
I guess that's what my heart needs too.
The good times are when the sun shines,
The tough times are when it's dark out.

Depression and anxiety,
Try to take over.
The stars begin to remind me,
That even in darkness...
There will always be light,
Even if it's faint.

Underneath the starlit sky,
My thoughts begin to wander.
If you weren't here,
People would notice...
For your life is precious.
Take life a day at a time,
And don't take it for granted.

The Broken Heart and Injured Soul

My heart has been broken,
While my soul was injured.
There may come a time,
When you think I'm unloveable.
Just know that if you leave,
My promises will be kept.
I don't go back on my word..
For I understand the value,
Of lifelong honesty.

My heart has been broken,
While my soul was injured.
I'm the one people like to replace...
Sometimes my heart and soul,
Are more fragile than you'd think.

If you want me to disappear,
Why come to my grave?
When my time comes,
To leave the earth...
Never forget that your actions,
Are echos to your words.
The pieces of my heart,
Try to come together...
While my soul is being mended.
The memories created,
Will forever remain.

Life Requires A Rainstorm

These eyes you see,
Shine bright...
Before each rainstorm.

During the rainstorm,
These eyes glisten...
While each tear falls,
Hitting the ground.
The rainstorms come,
To make us appreciate...
Each day we have.

Whether it's sunny or rainy,
Find the positives...
Instead of the negatives.
After the rainstorm,
You'll see a rainbow.
All rainbows require,
Sun and rain...
To bring them to life.

This smile you now see,
Is the rainbow that forms...
After the storm.

These eyes you see,
Shine bright...
Before each rainstorm.
You have the power,
To make each day great.

A Limited Supply of Time

Make the most,
Out of the time you have...
For you have a limited supply.
Time will only disappear quicker,
With each passing day.

You can ask what if questions,
All day long...
But they wouldn't get you far,
In this journey we call life.
Fear and doubt,
Cause us to worry...
More than we should.

Today wasn't guaranteed,
To arrive at all...
Just like tomorrow,
May never come.
Take a moment,
To be thankful...
For another day,
No matter what struggles...
May be present.

Make the most,
Out of the time you have...
For you have a limited supply.
Time will only disappear quicker,
With each passing day.

The Warning Signs

Warning signs known as red flags,
Will not always be easy to spot.
You shouldn't be a prisoner,
In any of your relationships.

No relationship is perfect,
So if you have to...
Remind the person,
That you're human too.

If you're hurting,
It's okay to dwell...
In your feelings for a bit,
Before asking for help.

In a relationship of any kind,
You shouldn't feel trapped...
Like you're gasping for air.
Your safety and happiness matter,
Don't let people tell you otherwise.
When you don't see the warning signs,
Or when you ignore the signs...
It can feel like you're being suffocated,
While your heart is shattering.

Warning signs known as red flags,
Will not always be easy to spot.
You shouldn't be a prisoner,
In any of your relationships.

A Lifetime of Memories

Step by step,
Day by day...
These moments turn,
Into memories.

There are times we want,
To remember things...
For the rest of our lives.
There are also times,
Where we want to forget...
Certain things that have happened.

Live today,
Like tomorrow...
Won't ever arrive.
Reflect on the past,
To learn from it...
Seeing that you grew,
From what life threw your way.
As we take our next breath...
Prepare for the future,
While living in the present.

Step by step,
Day by day...
Moments turn,
Into memories.

The Past Meets the Future

The future is hidden,
In the past.
In order to have,
A better tomorrow...
We must reflect,
On the past.

The future is hidden,
In the past.
When reflecting on the past,
Be careful not to get stuck...
For you must come back,
To the present.
It's easy to get lost,
In all that has happened...
For time has gone fast.

The future is hidden,
In the past.
As time goes on,
A new day begins...
While time goes by faster,
Making the days shorter.

The hourglass runs out of time,
After each 24 hours...
The future is hidden,
In the past.

The Landfill

My heart is not something,
That you can just break...
And take to the landfill.

I'm human just like you,
Even though you treat me...
As if I'm not.
One minute you're happy,
Then the next you're upset...
You say you love me,
While your actions...
Prove otherwise.
I'm not perfect,
For I'm human just like you...
I wish you'd see that.

My heart is not something,
That you can just break...
And take to the landfill.

Unexpected Events

Unexpected events,
Do happen...
Sometimes plans get altered.

When your mom didn't want you,
Planned to get an abortion...
Unil family changed her mind.
Being told you're worthless,
By the person...
You wanted love from the most,
Is heartbreaking.

Being called a mistake,
Makes it hard...
To see the value in life.
Wondering why,
You weren't wanted...
Is a painful process.
Open your eyes child,
See that you're loved...
By those around you.

It's okay to ask for help,
You're not alone my dear.
Your life is precious,
Never take a day for granted.
Things may be hard now,
But they won't be hard forever.
Being told you're worthless,
By the person...
You wanted love from the most,
Is heartbreaking.

Get Out Before it's too Late

In this journey we call life,
There can be toxic relationships...
Of any kind.

What we had was poisonous,
I'm glad I realized...
Before it was too late.
We stopped talking,
Since you decided...
You didn't want me around.
You claimed I was waste of space,
That I didn't deserve to live.

Now that I'm finally happy,
You suddenly realize...
How cruel you were.
Now that I'm happy,
You tell me you're sorry...
But your apology,
Means nothing...
Since it's not sincere.

You want me back in your life,
But you burned that bridge...
A long time ago,
So that'll never happen.
Just remember,
We said goodbye...
Instead of farewell.

A Thief's Punishment

You steal the hearts,
Of everyone you meet.

You're a thief,
That walks at night.
You're a thief that hides,
In broad daylight…
Scared you'll get caught.

You were a joker,
That found a lady…
Who wasn't a fool.

You can't always get away,
With breaking innocent hearts.

When you genuinely love someone,
The person becomes aware…
Of your next move,
For you gave them your heart.

You're a thief,
That walked at night.
You're a thief,
That hid in broad daylight…
Until you got caught,
When you fell in love…
With an honest heart.

The Speed Limit

Life doesn't have a speed limit,
For it goes fast at times…
Making it slow down,
At other moments.

We may not always know,
What will happen…
But the future,
Is hidden in the past…
So reflect and you'll find clues.

Each moment that's yet to come,
Is apart of the future…
That was never a mystery.

Life doesn't have a speed limit.

Each second that passes by,
Turns into history…
The code for each mystery.

Life doesn't have a speed limit,
For it goes fast at times…
Making it slow down,
At other moments.

Quilts

Quilts and blankets,
Are unique…
In their own ways.

Quilts are more,
Than a blanket…
For they're made by hand,
With a love that adds warmth…
Instead of something,
Being made at factory.

Quilts and blankets,
Are unique…
In their own ways.

Quilts take longer to make,
For they're more intricate.

Blankets take less time to make,
For they're usually made…
In a factory of sorts.

Quilts and blankets,
Are unique…
In their own ways.

Handmade Quilts,
Always tell a story…
For they were made with care.

Quilts are like people,
Because no two…
Will ever be the same.

Fear and Regret

Fear and regret,
Will try to stop you…
From being successful.
What's holding you back,
From following your dreams?
What's stopping you,
From smiling today?
Have fear and regret,
Taken over your life?

Fear and regret,
Will try to stop you…
From being successful.
Hope and faith,
Go hand in hand…
For it's hard to find,
One without the other.

A life well lived,
Is far more…
Than outside world can see.
A life well lived,
Is seen from within...
The heart, soul, and mind.
Fear and regret,
Will try to stop you...
From being successful.

The Memory Box

The time we spent together,
Along with the time apart...
Have created memories,
That will never be erased.
Ever since my first breath,
You held my hand...
Guiding me through,
Life's winding roads.
You always had my back,
Showing me you care...
If it wasn't for you,
I may never have had...
A life to even live.

The time we spent together,
Along with the time apart...
Have created memories,
That will never be erased.
Since God called you home,
I have felt lost without you here...
I just need to remember,
That you'll always be near...
For you left an everlasting mark,
On the world and those around you.
Now that you're in heaven,
The time we spent...
Together or apart,
Now mean much more...
Than I thought they did before.

The Chances Were Given

She gave you chance after chance,
Never wanting to give up on you…
For she gave you her heart.
There is only so much pain,
That a heart can handle…
Before someone walks away.
She gave you her love,
While you told her…
She would never be enough.
Once you think you've lost her,
You apologize…
Begging her to stay.
The girl will stay for a while,
Hoping you'll genuinely care.

You not only broke the girl's heart,
But you made her feel unloveable…
Making her want to disappear.
Eventually she stopped,
Giving you chances…
For she finally had enough of the abuse.
She gave you chance after chance,
Never wanting to give up on you…
For she gave you her heart.

One day you'll wish she had stayed...
While you showed her that she's worth it,
For now that she's gone you feel alone...
One day someone will treat her right.

A Cry For Help

For the longest time,
These melancholy feelings...
Tried to take over your life.

When you feel abandoned,
By the people you care about...
Your heart breaks,
While each day seems to get harder...
You're doing the best you can,
With the difficulties of life.

Open your eyes,
Realize you're alive...
Life will have ups and downs,
For that's part of the journey.

You're capable of getting through,
Anything life throws your way...
For you'll always be loved.

If people would look into your eyes,
Instead of at your smile...
They'd see the pain in your soul,
Along with your cry for help.

For the longest time,
These melancholy feelings...
Tried to take over your life.

The Heart that's in Pain

You try to hide your hurting heart,
From those closest to you...
For you're scared,
That you'll hurt them too.

You always put others first,
Forgetting that it's more than okay...
To take care of yourself too.
While you wear a smile,
You hope one person sees...
The tears wanting to fall,
From your eyes.

Your life hasn't been the easiest,
Some events hard to comprehend...
For the reason of why things happen,
Aren't always the easiest to see.

You try to hide your hurting heart,
From those closest to you...
For you're scared,
That you'll hurt them too.

Sometimes hiding your hurting heart,
Will hurt someone much more...
Than your honesty,
For they love and care for you.

The Silent Rush

The silence of the night,
Prepares us…
For the morning rush.
The darkness of the night,
Is lit up by the stars…
That eventually lead us,
To the sunshine of tomorrow.

The journey of life,
Has ups and downs…
Allowing us to grow,
Into who we're meant to be.
The silence of the night,
Prepares us…
For the morning rush.

The past has information,
That helps us prepare…
For the future,
While living in the moment...
Open your eyes,
See that your life matters.
The silence of the night,
Prepares us…
For the morning rush.

Pacing Back and Forth

Pacing back and forth,
Not knowing how…
To take the news,
For it broke my heart.

Now that you're in heaven,
Instead of here on earth…
Hearts are remembering you,
For you blessed the lives of others.

Your legacy will live on,
For death didn't end your story…
It created a new beginning for you,
You're finally home and no longer in pain.

Pacing back and forth,
Not knowing how…
To take the news,
For it broke my heart.

We may not be able to see each other,
But I know you'll always be here…
Holding my hand,
Watching over those you loved.

An Adventure in the Sky

After every sunset,
Comes a sunrise.
The sun shows its face,
Until it's time…
For the moon and stars,
To make their appearance.

After every sunset,
Comes a sunrise.
When you keep your head down,
It becomes harder to find…
The beautiful things,
This world has to offer.

After every sunset,
Comes a sunrise.
When you lift your head up,
Remaining hopeful…
The beauties of the earth,
Will been seen with a clear view.

After every sunset,
Comes a sunrise.
Times may be difficult,
With life's ups and downs...
For we are like butterflies,
We start out as caterpillars...
Before we get the chance,
To spread our wings and fly.

The End

Life with you had been wonderful,
I knew your time would come…
But I didn't know when,
For that's something unpredictable.

I held your hand,
Until it went cold…
I stayed by your side,
Until the end.

Now that your time has arrived,
I wonder if you knew…
How much you were loved,
By each heart that your soul touched.

You left a mark on the world,
That no one can erase…
For your heart,
Was honest and kind...
Which gave people hope,
Allowing them to rejoice.

I knew your time would come,
But I didn't know when.

I held your hand,
Until it went cold…
I stayed by your side,
Until the end when you said farewell.

The Grieving Process

Heaven may seem far away,
When missing loved ones.
Heaven is closer than you realize,
For signs will be given to you…
That your loved ones,
Will always be by your side.
Death may seem like the end,
But each mark on the world…
And God's open arms tell us otherwise.

We may not physically be able,
To see all of our loved ones…
For some passed away,
But if we look to the sky…
Remaining hopeful,
We'll see signs…
That our hand is being held,
And that we'll never be alone.

Times may be tough,
And we may need time to grieve…
But we mustn't forget to remember,
All of the memories that were created…
Before time ran out.
Heaven may seem far away,
When missing loved ones.
Heaven is closer than you realize,
For signs will be given to you…
That your loved ones,
Will always be by your side.

Life's Achievements

Great things won't happen,
If you hold back.
Great things will happen,
When you do your best.

Success won't come,
Unless you occasionally fail.
When failure happens,
It opens the doorway to success.

When you feel alone,
Remember this…
You'll always have,
Someone by your side…
For God would never,
Abandon you.

No one ever said,
That life's journey…
Would be easy.

If you're holding back,
Not making the most…
Out of each day,
What are you achieving?

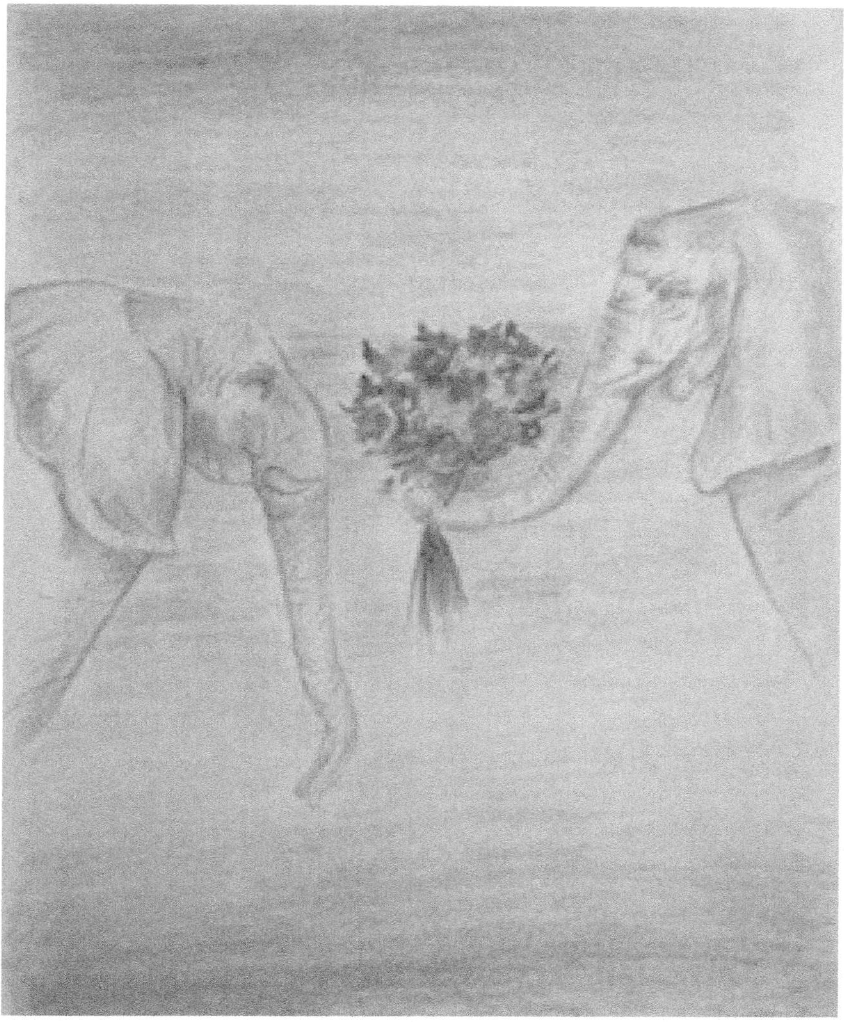

Part Two

The Homeless Heart

My home completely disappeared,
The day that you passed away.

Now that you're gone,
My heart is heavy…
Wishing that we could of had,
At least one more minute together.

My heart became homeless,
When you went up to heaven.

The pain was unbearable,
Until I saw signs…
That you would always,
Be by my side.

Now that I know,
You'll always be near…
My heart's keeping its beat,
For it knows you won't disappear.

You made sure I was given a chance,
For you thought my life was worth fighting for.

My home had completely disappeared,
The day that you passed away…
For I felt lost and alone,
Until I looked to God...
Asking him to lead my heart home,
Where it belongs.

Sacrifices

When it comes to our freedom,
It can be easy…
To take it for granted.

We aren't free by chance,
For men and women…
Sacrifice their lives,
To protect our country.

Men and women,
Died on the battlefield…
Trying to protect you and I.
Not everyone dies in battle,
But they do risk…
Their lives for us.

We aren't free by chance,
For men and women…
Sacrifice their lives,
To protect our country.

When saying thank you,
To a veteran…
Remember that if it wasn't for them,
Our country wouldn't be free.

Time Creates Our Memories

The life we live on earth,
Will soon come to an end…
The clock is ticking,
Turning every second into a memory.

The mark we leave,
Lives on…
Through the people,
That we knew.

Once our time is up,
There's no going back.

Did you live the life you wanted?

Did you make the most,
Out of your time on earth?

What will you be remembered for?

The life we live on earth,
Will soon come to an end…
The clock is ticking,
Turning every second into a memory.

The Lost Soul

Getting lost is fairly easy,
In today's world...
While finding your soul,
Is simpler than it was in the past.

Finding your way,
From here or there...
May not be the easiest,
Especially in new places.

The world is full,
Of people and activities.

When part of the universe,
Is asleep...
The other part is awake.

The sun goes down,
Allowing the moon and stars...
To come out.

The sun rises,
While the moon and stars...
Rest in our hearts,
Allowing a new day to start.

Getting lost is fairly easy,
In today's world...
While finding your soul,
Is simpler than it was in the past.

The Heart and The Clock

Whatever is unknown,
Will soon be revealed.

The future is coming,
The past and present...
Are leading us to it.

All that is currently known,
Will never go back...
To hiding in the area,
Of the unknown.

The clock of the world,
Won't stop...
For the world,
Will continue to spin.

Heartbeats are like alarm clocks,
For when time on earth is up...
It stops or goes off letting us know.

Whatever is unknown,
Will soon be revealed.

Your time on earth is limited,
How will you spend it?

When your time is up,
Will you be happy...
With the mark you left?

Finding Rest

Hearts catch fire,
When toxic people…
Take over.

The human heart,
Becomes a jail cell…
When toxic situations,
Let negativity take over.

With God's guidance and grace,
The fire in each heart…
Is put to rest—
Allowing the heart's jail cell,
To finally disappear.

When a heart is at rest,
Peace is found…
Which allows positivity,
To chase away any negativity.

Trusting God's word,
Is key to find peace…
For he makes each heart whole,
Never abandoning the world.

If you had one wish,
What would it be?

I Only Want What's Best For You

When I'm singin the blues,

You must listen closely...

For each happy note,

That I happen to stick in.

Each note that I sing,

Reveals the pain—

Along with the joy...

That life has given me.

With each new tune,

That my heart sings...

I hope that someday—

It may benefit you,

For life is a mixture...

Of pain and joy,

And I only want...

What's best for you.

The Light that Shines

The sun and moon,
Shine their light…
On the world.

The sun and moon,
Come at different hours…
For the sun comes out at daytime,
While the moon comes out at nighttime.

The sun is accompanied,
By the clouds or blue skies.
The moon is accompanied,
By the twinkling stars.

The sun and moon,
Shine their light…
On the world.

Life is like the sky...
For there's sunny days,
Along with darker days.

When life combines,
Sun and rain…
Or good and bad,
A rainbow is formed.

The sun and moon,
Shine their light…
On the world.

The Holiday Season

The Holiday Season,
Brings the world cheer…
Making me wish,
That you were still here.

Through the holiday cheer,
The people begin to hear…
A new year approaching,
Which calls for toasting.

The Holiday Season…
Brings the world cheer,
Reminding me…
You'll always be here,
No matter what time of year.

You may not be here physically,
But you're here in spirit…
Your mark will never be erased.

A season for meeting,
Allows the heart to hear…
Bells ringing and people singing,
For the end of the year is near.

The Holiday Season,
Brings the world cheer…
Giving each soul hope,
Chasing away fear.

When Home is Found

There's a difference between,
A house and a home.

Each house you see,
Is a place that wishes…
To someday be a home.

Every home you see,
Is far from being…
A cookie cutter place.

A house has four walls,
Along with a roof.

In a home you feel peace,
For there's love and warmth.

Home doesn't have to be a place,
For it can be someone's embrace.

There's a difference between,
A house and a home.

Through the good and bad times,
The place called home…
Can never be replaced,
For home is where your heart leads you.

The Thankful Glimpse

When the two of us,
Were first introduced…

I new that my reality,
Was about to change.

When he looked at me,
I for once felt beautiful…

Since he was genuine,
And I could tell…

That he wasn't going,
To try and change me.

When our eyes met,
He made me see…

Who I wanted to be.

He tore down my walls,
And stole my heart…

Leaving me defenseless,
And at a loss for words.

In that moment I prayed,
Asking the Lord…

To make this last forever,
Since he touched my soul…

In a way no one could see,
And I didn't want anything to end.

The Lord answered my prayer,
When he declared us as one…

For true love stories,
Aren't included with an ending.

For the rest of my life,
It will always be him and I…

Hand in hand,
With God on our side…

Giving the world a glimpse,
Of what thankfulness looks like.

One Life Left to Live

The seconds will pass you by,
Making each minute arrive…
Only for an hour to appear,
For a new day is in the making.

Today will pass you by,
Leading you to tomorrow…
Making each day end.

The sun will rise,
The sun will set…
Just like moments,
Turn into memories.

Are you lost in your imagination?
Are you stuck in reality?
What is the purpose of life?

When treasuring each moment,
The seconds and minutes...
Pass by a little quicker,
While sometimes passing by slower.

Make the most out of your time,
For you only have one life to live…
Here on earth,
Don't let it pass you by.

The Fragile Heart

Some scars can be seen through the eyes,
While some are hidden inside…
Where only a caring heart can find,
The scars that aren't seen by the eye.

Scars come in all shapes and sizes,
They help make us who we are…
Don't let them stop your dreams,
From coming true.

Hearts can be fragile,
For they've been broken…
People may put a wall,
Around their fragile heart…
In hopes to protect it,
From getting broken again.

When someone is around,
The right people…
The fragile heart is stronger now,
Than it ever was in the past.

Not everyone is a villain,
For some people are kind souls.

Let the song of your life play,
Through the highs and lows…
Even if a few beats are skipped.

Take My Heart

No one can take,
The place you hold…
In my heart,
For you're the reason…
That this heart of mine,
Keeps its beat.

The distance is hard,
For I miss you…
The second we separate.

One day we won't,
Have to say goodnight…
For the distance,
Will eventually be gone.

I hope you know,
Just how special you are...
For you're my whole world.

Without you I'd be homeless.
Without you my heart,
Would lose its beat…
For you're the reason,
Its beat has stayed strong.

No one can take your place,
For you hold my heart…
In the palm of your hands.

The Puzzle of Life

Every day that passes by,
Is apart of the puzzle called life.

Every second and every minute,
Are the pieces used…
To put the puzzle together.

Yesterday was added to the puzzle,
While today's puzzle piece…
Will be added once the day is complete.

The puzzle of life,
Will forever grow…
For tomorrow,
Is a possibility.

What are you missing?
What will your puzzle,
Look like in the end?
What mark are you leaving,
On the world?

The mark your leave,
Is a permanent one…
Will you be satisfied,
With the one you've left?

Every day that passes by,
Is apart of the puzzle called life.

Letting Love Find You

Searching for love,
Won't get you far…
For it's meant to find you,
Instead of the other way around.

This journey of life,
Is accompanied…
By God himself,
For he'll never abandon you.

When you stop trying…
To hunt down love,
It allows you to grow…
Blossoming into,
Who you're meant to be.

When you're ready,
To find your soulmate…
That love will find you.

When love is found,
There's no room for doubt…
For if it's true,
It won't hide from you.

Searching for love,
Won't get you far…
For it's meant to find you,
Instead of the other way around.

The Last Day

This day on earth,
Could be your last…
For tomorrow,
May never arrive.

If tomorrow appears,
Then it may be your last day...
Since we aren't guaranteed,
A certain amount of days on earth.

Yesterday is now a memory,
That helps you…
Live in the present,
While preparing for tomorrow.
Our time on earth is limited,
While life in heaven…
Is something that lasts forever.

The time we have alive,
Will eventually be gone…
Only allowing our mark,
To stay behind on earth.

Your actions are,
The echo to your words.

This day on earth,
Could be your last…
What impact will you,
Decide to leave?

Escaping the Cold

Looking for an escape,
From this cold cruel world...
Just wanting to belong.

Hiding spots are all around,
None of them quite right...
They say that I matter,
But why do I?

I'm just another person,
Trying to make it...
Through another day,
Like everyone else.

When will I truly belong?

This world needs to trust God,
For when it doesn't...
The peace feels like it's gone,
Making the world a cold cruel place.

The Choice Is Yours

Dreams wish to become reality,
While reality wishes…
To be a dream come true.

A dream can only,
Collide with reality…
When hard work and effort,
Are put into both.

Yesterday is gone,
Which leaves us today…
To fight for,
What we believe in.

Dreams and reality,
Are two separate things…
Until you turn your life,
Into a dream come true.

Each wish your heart makes,
Echoes inside your soul...
Begging your mind,
To do what it takes...
To turn dreams and reality,
Into the same thing.

Finally you have the choice,
To let your dreams and reality collide…
For hard work always pays off.

Forever Dancing Together

She found light,
From his darkness...
While he found darkness,
From her light.

Darkness and light,
Always find each other...
For they make a great team.

Without the darkness,
The light wouldn't see...
Its full potential.

Without the light,
The darkness...
Would be powerless.

Everywhere you look,
There will be...
Light and darkness,
For they both help us grow...
Allowing sadness and happiness,
To dance forever in our soul.

The heart and soul,
Have a mind of their own...
For they use light and darkness,
To create something meaningful.

The Final Hug

Tears fall from my eyes,
For my heart aches…
To see you again.

You lived each day,
Like it was your last…
You turned a house,
Into a home…
Making each heart full.

Trying to keep,
Melancholy feelings…
From taking over life,
For you deserve to be celebrated.

I know you're in heaven,
Which is comforting…
Although if I had one more hug,
It would help ease the pain…
For it'll be awhile,
Until I see you again.

Your mark on the world,
Will forever live on…
For you'll always be loved and missed.

Tears fall from my eyes,
For my heart aches…
To see you again.

I Asked God Why

I really wanted,

To have at least...

One more second with you,

Before God took you...

Away from your earthly home,

And brought you to heaven.

I know I shouldn't,

Be greedy with time...

But your goodbye,

Broke my heart.

I miss you now,

Just like I've missed you...

Ever since,

You became my guardian angel.

No matter how much time passes,

I'll always miss you...

For you played,

A major role in my life.

I wish I could of had,

More time with you...

Before you traveled,

Up to your heavenly home.

Some days without you here,

Are more painful than others...

But no matter how the day goes,

I'll always wish...

That heaven had visiting hours,

Or a line I could call...

Even just to hear you say hello.

I still silently ask God,

Why you had to go so soon...

Because this life of mine,

Isn't the same without you.

When my time comes,

And I get to see you again...

I hope you know,

That I'll run to you...

And that you may see me cry,

Because it'll be good...

To finally be,

Back by your side.

Washing Away the Pain

My heart aches today,
For the pain is hard...
To wash away.

A broken heart,
Requires the soul...
To be mended.

The mind tries to lead,
The heart and soul...
Even though,
They drift apart.

Each day alive,
Joy and sadness...
End up colliding.

Easy journeys,
Find difficult journeys...
Turning them both,
Into something beautiful.

If I do not wake up,
Please remember...
My life was lived fully,
Thanks to all of you.

My heart aches today,
For the pain is hard...
To wash away.

The Bells That Ring

The lights and decorations,
Are inside and outside…
A place called home.

The fireplace warms the soul,
While seeing loved ones…
Touches the heart.

The presence of loved ones,
That are in heaven…
Will forever linger,
For their mark was made.

The snow falls and the sun shines,
Letting the cheerful times...
Hide the melancholy feelings,
For holidays are magical and healing.

Some people reminisce about old times,
While others dance and sing…
For bells continue to ring,
Spreading holiday cheer.

This time of year is a special one...
Where the memories created,
Will always remain…
Until it's time,
To reflect on the past…
For the past is the key,
To a brighter future.

The Life That Is Given

Your name is forever engraved,
On this heart of mine...
For you gave me life.

Your love is given to the world,
For your people...
Are important and special.

Your love isn't earned from labor,
For you died on the cross...
To save us from our sins,
Never allowing us to be abandoned.

A name that is above all others,
Will forever be yours...
For your embrace is all,
That the world truly needs.

Without praising you,
In the good and bad times...
We'd have cold hearts,
For we don't always see...
Everything that you envision,
For you're our savior.

Your name is forever engraved,
On this heart of mine...
For you gave me life.

A New Beginning

Dead end roads,
Often lead…
To new beginnings.

Even when a door is closed,
There is still a window…
For you'll never be trapped,
With God by your side.

Each chapter of life,
Comes to an end…
So new adventures can start.

Each breath you take,
Is precious…
For you are only guaranteed,
The moment you're in now…
Along with life in heaven,
If you allowed God into your heart.

Each chapter of life,
Comes to an end…
So new adventures can start.

Focusing on material things,
Won't let you get far…
For the bigger aspects of life,
Always come from the heart.

The Key of Life

The key to living life fully,
Is to have hope…
No matter what's going on,
In the journey called life.

Sometimes the mind gets cloudy,
While the heart gets lost…
Making it hard to decipher,
Right from wrong.

Dreams and reality are related,
For if hard work is put into a dream...
Then it becomes reality.

If a dream lacks hard work,
Then it will stay a dream…
Making reality difficult to grasp.

With a clouded mind and lost heart,
You mustn't forget where you came from…
Use your roots to assist you,
With finding your way.

The key to a successful life...
Is to understand that failure,
Is a stepping stone that's needed...
To get from where you are now,
To where you wish to be.

As the seasons change,
The weather begins…
To be different than before.

Believe

As the weather changes,
Life begins to drift…
In another direction,
For no one can stay put forever.

As the holidays arrive,
People tend to thrive…
For cheer is in the air,
Lifting up sad hearts.

Positivity and negativity…
Are neighbors,
Both so different from each other…
For one is kind,
While the other is harmful.

When today ends,
Will you be ready for tomorrow…
Or will you be stuck in the past?

Miracles and blessings…
Happen every day,
You just have to believe…
For hope is formed,
From good and bad situations.

Tending the Garden

The heart and soul...
Is a garden,
For without proper care...
Weeds begin to take over.

When weeds take over,
The nurtured plants...
Start to wither away,
Until the gardener comes back...
To tend to the crops.

The heart and soul grow most,
When the brain takes the lead...
For when the mind is lost,
Unhealthy thoughts take over...
Making positivity harder to find,
In the darker times of life.

The heart and soul,
Are produce of the mind...
For without the brain,
The heart and soul would be lost.

Life is full of ups and downs,
So ask yourself this...
Are you willing to take care,
Of yourself with God's guidance...
Or will you wallow in self pity,
When things don't go your way?
What will you do to help someone in need?
What will you do to make the world a better place?
What will your mark on the world be?

The Tears of Remembrance

When my time on earth is done,
If you shed a tear or two...
Know that they are raindrops,
Making room for a rainbow...
To appear in your heart,
For we'll never be apart.

You may mourn,
Claiming that my life was cut short,
For you wanted more time...
Don't let the distance,
Shatter your heart.
The life I have lived on earth,
Will live on through you...
For the dash between,
My birth date and death date...
Proclaim that I made a mark.

The sun had a light that shines,
Brighter than anything ever seen...
Now the raindrops try to wash away,
The sorrow and melancholy feelings.

It may be hard to smile now,
Just remember to celebrate...
The times we had,
Instead of being heartbroken...
That my heart stopped beating,
For we'll meet again someday.
This is farewell and not goodbye,
For we'll never be apart—
Since I'll always be in your heart.

The Carolers Message

When the carolers sing,
Silent night…

My heart begins to cry,
For you're not by my side.

When the carolers sing,
Joy to the world…

I think of how,
You're with Jesus now.

When the carolers sing,
The Hallelujah Chorus…
reminded that hope,
Longs to be held onto.

When the carolers sing,
Santa Claus is coming to town…

I am fully reminded,
That not everyone…
Knows what Christmas,
Is really about.

No matter how many,
Songs the carolers sing…

I will continue,
Making trips down memory lane.

No matter how cold,
The world may be…

The thought of you,
And the Lord's love…
Are what keep,
My heart beating.

Throughout this time of year,
One thing is always made clear…

And that's the fact that loved ones,
Are always near and never far…

For their presence will never disappear,
Since God turned them into Guardian Angels.

The Lifestyle

Watching the days go by,
Turning into months and years...
Wondering why time has to fly by,
So very quickly.

One day childhood turns,
Into something called adulthood.

Growing up,
Won't always be required...
For our hearts will forever,
Have room for the inner child.

Everyone has different lifestyles,
Allowing different marks...
To be made on the world.

Time flies by quicker,
Than desired...
Making it vital,
To treasure every moment.

Once each moment,
Becomes a memory...
While life seems to flash,
Right before...
My very eyes,
Making an earthly life...
Seem so short,
For time never stops flying.

The Pain that Lingers

You hide your feelings,
From the people in your life…
For you're scared that if they knew,
Everyone would leave.

You built a wall around your heart,
Not allowing anyone in…
For you've been betrayed before,
Making you have a heavy heart.

Hiding melancholy feelings,
Behind a smile won't work…
When someone loves you,
For they'll see the pain…
That lingers in your eyes,
Just begging for…
A genuine soul to comfort you.

No matter what is happening,
In your journey of life…
A hand will always be,
There for you to hold…
For you'll never be alone,
No matter how abandoned you feel.

Open your heart and soul,
Allow yourself to see…
That not everyone,
Is a villain…
For you'll always be loved and cared for.

The Decorated Town

All around town,
Christmas decorations...
Are all that can be seen.

Holiday festivities,
Are for you and me...
For the choirs sing,
At this late hour...
While the bells ring,
Every so often.

All around town,
Christmas decorations...
Are all that can be seen,
While music plays...
Reminding people,
To remember...
What holidays are,
Truly all about.

Each holiday without loved ones,
May be extremely difficult...
Until you open your heart,
To the fact that they'll always...
Celebrate with you,
For they're still in your heart.

Your loved ones in heaven,
Will forever live on...
As long as you remember them.

A Life Above the Clouds

I'm human,
Which means…
That I make mistakes,
While occasionally getting lost.

The people in the world,
May know my name…
Although no one,
Knows me better than you God.

Without you lord,
I'd be lost and fearful…
You lead me through,
The hills and the valleys…
You lead me through,
The sunny days and the storms…
You lead me through,
The ups and downs.

Your love amazes me,
For when I feel unworthy…
You remind me that I am worthy.
If at times I feel alone,
You remind me…
That you'll always be,
By my side.

The lord will always be with you.
Your loved ones in heaven,
Will forever watch over you.

When Fear Takes Over

Living a life of fear,
Can make you wish…
That you'd disappear.

Living in a world,
So full of hate…
Makes it hard to see,
That it's also filled with love.

A life filled with fear,
Won't get you far...
Or anywhere near,
Where your dreams…
Tend to take you,
For fear is harmful.

No matter how hard,
Find a reason to smile…
Even if it takes,
Every ounce of effort you have.

Living a life of fear,
Can make you wish…
That you'd disappear.

A Dance in Heaven

When the time comes,
For me to say I do…
You won't be here,
To give me away.
When the time comes,
For the father daughter dance…
I'll remember how,
You were always more…
Of father figure than a grandfather.

We were extremely close,
Even though you're in heaven…
While I'm here on earth,
Our bond still stands strong.
When the time comes,
For me to say I do…
You won't be here,
To give me away…
For you're in a better place,
I just hope you're proud…
For I finally found,
A love like the one…
That was found in,
You and my sweet grandmother.

You both will forever have…
A place in my heart,
I just wish you were for when…
The time comes,
For me to say I do…
I hope the two of you,
Have a dance in heaven.

Celebrating Forever

The sea is a midnight blue,

And the stars shine...

For me and you.

As I think about life,

And the memories...

We've made,

It makes me smile.

I was taught,

That even when...

Distance tries to separate,

Two people...

It will never succeed,

If they're truly in love...

And I learned,

That we mustn't forget...

That God has a plan,

Even if...

At times,

It's hard to understand.

True love looks,

To the lighthouse within...

And the stars up above,

Because when the love is real...

The two hearts,

Are transformed into one.

True love is never ending,

And God brought us together...

So here's a toast,

To our forever!

The Agenda

The pace of your mind,
Is either faster or slower…
Than the beat of your heart.

Your heart and mind,,
Go at their own pace…
For they're not in a race.

Your heart and soul,
May not always…
Have the same agenda,
That your mind has...
Since two different paths,
Require different paces.

The beat of you heart,
Goes along to the rhythm…
Of your soul,
While your mind…
Is in sync,
With the past and present.

Let your spirit soar,
Guiding you to the future…
For you'll always have,
A guardian angel.

The pace of your mind,
Is either faster or slower…
Than the beat of your heart.

A Decision for the Lord and Me

The world constantly,
Tries to tell me...
Who I should be,
And that's not right.

I am who I am,
And that's not a crime...
So like me or hate me,
As I turn my dreams into reality.

The world wants me,
To do a copy and paste...
Because they want to decide,
What I look like...
And they want to tell me,
Who I am on the inside.

I am who I am,
And that's not a crime...
I like opinions and suggestions,
On how to improve daily...
But I won't let these bullies and haters,
Get me down or crush my spirit.

So a message to the world,
That's trying to tell me...
Who I should be,
I hope you know...
That who I'm truly meant to be,
Is a decision for the Lord and me.

A Smile Meets the Storm

The daylight calls,
For the heart...
To be saved.

The darkness of the night,
Calls for the light of the stars...
To shine out through each soul.

Sometimes as people,
We want to close our eyes...
Hoping that when they open,
The storms of life won't be there.

We the people,
Will sometimes fake a smile...
For we'd rather not explain,
The reason we are sad.

When a person is filled,
With empathy and compassion...
They learn to make eye contact,
Instead of always believing a smile...
For it could be a mask.

What will tomorrow hold?
Are you stuck,
Hitting replay on the past?
Are you ready,
For what's to come in the future?

Who I'm Meant To Be

I may be plus size,
But that doesn't mean...
That you should body shame me,
And my size doesn't mean...
That I can't be,
Beautiful too.

I may have ups and downs,
But that's all apart of life...
And I'll never let my looks,
Take over my personality.

What matters most,
Or what should matter most...
Is what comes from within,
Since true beauty is found there.

No one is exactly the same,
For we're all different sizes...
And most of us look different.

You and I may have similarities,
But you are you and I am me...
So you can either like me or hate me,
But I'll always be who I'm meant to be.

Hope Begins to Bloom

When happiness turns,
Into melancholy feelings...
That's when hope blooms.

A lost soul is,
A heartbeat...
That loses control,
While the mind wishes...
For healing and comfort,
Instead of pain and suffering.

When happiness turns,
Into melancholy feelings...
That's when hope blooms.

There are critics in the world,
That will try to tear people down...
More than they already are.

A broken heart leads to,
A soul that becomes lost...
While the mind,
Must try to lead them.

When happiness turns,
Into melancholy feelings...
That's when hope blooms.

Going Separate Ways

A family sometimes,
Gets separated...
Due to certain situations.

When separations occur,
Hearts get broken...
Requiring each soul,
To be mended.

Relationships don't,
Always last...
For not everyone,
Has good intentions.

When a relationship,
Is meant to last...
Honesty and trust,
Along with loyalty...
Won't be hard to find,
For communication is key.

When separations occur,
Hearts get broken...
Requiring each soul,
To be mended.

When you find your soulmate,
There will be no room for doubt...
For what's meant to last,
Won't end with God's guidance.

An Angel on Earth

My life has fallen to pieces,
Since you passed away...
For my heart got shattered,
Into pieces...
Crushing my soul,
Making me lose my mind.

Now that you're in heaven...
I don't know what to do,
I just long for your embrace.
Since the day you left,
I replay the memories made...
For that's the only way,
I can see you...
Until it becomes,
My time to leave earth.

I hope that one day,
I'll make you proud.

My life had fallen to pieces...
When you passed away,
Until I learned to accept...
That while you may be in heaven,
A piece of you will always live on...
Through everyone you met,
For you were an angel on earth...
Who eventually had to leave,
To join Jesus at his feet.

A Life of Comprehension

They say I'll be missed,
When my time to leave earth…
Finally arrives.
I'm losing the power to keep fighting,
For depression keeps weighing me down…
Making life seem so dull,
While I wonder how much time…
I actually have left.

It's hard to comprehend,
What people see in me…
For I see so many flaws.
I will never see myself,
The way that others see me…
But now I know that,
God loves me and my flaws.

The lord has a purpose for my life,
When depression tries to tear me apart…
I know it's okay to cry,
I know it's okay to be upset…
I just need to always remember,
That I'll never be alone.
Jesus will always hold my hand,
For he loves me just like he loves you…
For we'll always mean the world to him.

They say I'll be missed when my time,
To leave earth finally arrives…
But the memories that were made,
Will always linger in the hearts of those I knew.

A Families Love

Family isn't a term,
That requires...
People to be,
Blood related.

My family is more,
Than people...
That I'm related to,
For the heart decides...
Who truly is,
Apart of my family.

Family can consist of,
Friends and relatives...
While some people,
Marry into a family.

Some families separate,
While others grow closer…
A true family,
Won't abandon you...
For if they care,
They'll show it.

Family isn't a term,
That requires...
People to be,
Blood related.

A World of Inspiration

Inspiration comes,
From other people…
Along with,
What the world has to offer.

Without people being inspired,
Where would the world be?

What would the world be like,
If people had less motivation…
To get things done?

Success will never be achieved,
Until failure is experienced…
For without failure,
Success would not exist.

If you have a dream,
It can become reality…
If you put effort into it,
For with God by your side…
You have the power,
To get through…
Any obstacles,
Life throws your way.

Inspiration comes,
When it's least expected…
For it helps you see,
What truly matters.

Questioning Life

I'm living a life,
That doesn't...
Make sense.

Why live a life,
That involves pain?
Why can't life,
Always go as planned?

We the people,
Think that if life...
Didn't have pain,
It would be better.
We the people,
Think that if life...
Went as we planned it,
Happiness would stick around.

Without enduring pain,
Joy and happiness...
Wouldn't bloom,
For the good times...
Are what develop,
From the bad times.

Life refuses to go...
The way we want it to,
For God knows...
What's right for us,
Since he is our shepherd.

Holding Onto Hope

When a heart is shattered,
It often leads…
To a crushed soul,
Which makes it…
Harder to think clearly,
Or even remain faithful.

When you have a shattered heart,
Along with a crushed soul…
It becomes vital,
To hold onto hope.
Without remaining hopeful,
Life may seem meaningless…
For your head is in the clouds,
Just longing for an escape…
From the pain that leads you,
To joy and happiness that's yet to be seen.

While it may be easy to give up,
Please remember that it's okay…
To cry when life gets hard,
Then afterwards…
Try to lift your head up,
For even in the darkness…
Light is still found,
Making you into the person you are.

When a heart and soul,
Get broken into pieces…
It eventually gets mended,
By loved ones including God.

A Wandering Mind

As I lay awake at night,
Thoughts keep me awake...
For that's when reflections of life,
Usually make their appearance.

As I lay awake at night...
My mind wanders,
Through memory lane...
For during the day,
Hard work is done...
Preventing my mind,
From going astray.

When I finally fall asleep,
Dreams begin to form...
So that way when I awaken,
I have the choice to make it reality.

I must decide if my dreams,
Shall become reality...
For if I decide,
To let them remain dreams...
I may regret it,
So I must use my past...
To help me prepare for the future,
While God's guidance...
Allows me to live in the moment,
Valuing each breath I'm given.

Uncovering the Truth

The soul combines with the mind,
Allowing a person to show...
Their true colors,
In the sun and rain.

Art comes from the heart,
For it shows emotion...
That may be hard,
For someone to talk about.

Your voice is heard...
Through simplicity,
Along with creativity...
For personality,
Comes from within.

Your actions are,
The echo to your words...
Which cannot be silenced,
For once you make a mark...
On the world,
It will forever remain.

Your true colors,
Can be hidden...
Behind a smile,
Until your eyes…
Start to reveal,
How you truly feel.

When Bedtime Arrives

It's time for bed,
Lay down and rest...
For tomorrow,
Is on its way here.

Today went by,
Faster or slower...
Than imagined,
Since time either...
Flies by or seems,
To be hardly moving.

Reflecting on the past...
Tends to keep people awake,
Until their heavy eyelids...
Can't take it anymore,
Forcing them to get sleep.

Nightmares come,
When you least expect it...
Sometimes causing you,
To scream or jolt awake.
Nightmares do not,
Always happen...
Which may make them,
Seem more real...
Than they actually are,
For some are hard to forget.

No matter how well you sleep,
When you awaken...
You have the power,
To decide what becomes reality...
Along with what stays a dream,
For this is your life...
So you may as well,
Make the most out of it.

The Silent Scream

Will you be there for me,
When life gets hard...
Or will you disappear,
Until things get easier?

If you say you care,
I'll be able to tell if it's true...
Through your actions,
Since words become silent...
When your actions don't match up.

My trust is something that's earned,
For my heart has been hurt...
So it takes safety precautions,
To try to keep the past from repeating itself.
Some days I wish I could relive...
While others I wish I could forget.

The past is where,
Memories are located...
That can be reflected on,
While I'm living in the present...
For my future requires me,
To learn from the past.

If you want to keep me around,
There's something I must know...
Will you be there for me,
When life gets hard...
Or will you disappear,
Until things get easier?

Making A Wise Decision

At some point in our lives,
There comes a time...
When decisions,
Must be made.

Will you say yes or no?
Will you stay true to yourself,
Or will you try to be...
Like everyone else?
Are you happy,
With the way...
Life is turning out?

If you're lost in melancholy feelings,
What will you do...
To improve this difficult situation?

Every day decisions get made,
Some with positive results...
Others with negative ones,
But in the end...
How you react to what happens,
Is the most important.

At some point in our lives,
We must make decisions...
Some are harder,
Than others...
So when the time comes,
Choose wisely.

A Journey to the Light

Pain is felt,
Most deeply…
In the heart.

At times we may wish to ignore,
What the heart has to say…
But when we do,
The feeling of doom…
Has a tendency,
To make it feel…
Like hope is gone,
Making joy hard to see.

Hope will never...
Truly disappear,
For God's grace...
Will always lead us,
To the light...
Which is most powerful,
In the storm of life.

Pain is not permanent,
It's a stepping stone…
To help people grasp,
What matters most.

Pain is felt most deeply,
In the heart of you and I…
For it helps us see,
Who we're meant to be.

Life's Luxuries

Each day alive is a luxury,
No matter how rich or poor...
A person happens to be,
For the fact that life is a gift.

If you have shelter that feels like home,
Along with food and water...
That means you have a great deal of wealth.
If you add people that support you into the mix,
You're the richest you could be...
Since being wealthy and rich doesn't mean money,
It means finding acceptance in every situation...
Making the most out of what you have.

There will be days that make you want to give up,
Along with days that make you glad...
You had decided to stay longer.

Life is a series of hills and valleys...
Some of which we have to get through,
Alone with God until the world...
Needs to lend a helping hand,
For the lord is our shepherd.

Each day alive is a luxury,
No matter how rich or poor...
A person happens to be,
For the fact that life is a gift.

Finding a Place to Hide

My life began to flash,
Before my eyes...
When I tried to speak,
About everything unsaid...
For my time was almost up.

Things were left unsaid,
So now I have to choose...
What is most important,
Since I decided to...
Procrastinate until now.
Don't make the same mistakes,
That I made over the years—
Unless you want regret...
To follow you to the end of time.

If you have something to say,
Waste no time at all and make sure...
That heart and mind are heard,
For your life will flash before your eyes,
Making you wish time didn't go by so fast.

If you forget me please remember this,
Live your life instead of trying to hide...
Behind wanting to fit in,
For your life has a purpose...
So let your true colors show,
For you give meaning...
To this thing that we call life.

The Transformation

When your heart is weighed down,
From everything that surrounds you...
It puts your mind under pressure.

Sorting through the events of the day,
Can help you see clearly...
Preparing you for the future,
For each second counts.

When you live in the past,
You remain stuck...
Not moving forward,
To where you want to be...
The memories of the past,
Are stepping stones...
That will lead you,
To happiness and success.

Life will not always be easy,
For if it was simple you wouldn't grow,
So life tests you at times...
In order to allow you,
To transform into who you're meant to be.

When your heart is weighed down,
From everything that surrounds you...
It puts your mind under pressure,
Until you have learned...
To tell the difference between,
What truly matters and what doesn't.

Messages from the Heart

The world keeps trying,
To tell me who to be...
So I listen to suggestions,
About how to be a better person...
Since there is always,
Room for improvement.

The world may try to silence,
What my heart wishes to say...
So my actions have to match,
What my words express.

As the world tries to push me around,
Wanting me to be a cookie cutter image...
I try to help everyone understand,
The importance of not fitting in with a crowd.

My life's journey has made me who I am...
So I won't let the world force me into being,
The person that they wish me to be...
For my heart has dealt with pain and heartbreak,
So I have scars that aren't always...
Able to be seen by the world,
For I'm more than my appearance.

The world will keep trying to tell me who to be,
Until they finally learn that I am truly happy...
With being the person that I am,
No matter what life throw my way...
For the lord is with me every step of the way,
Since he'll always be my shepherd.

True Love's Embrace

My heart aches to be with you,
Each and every day…
For you complete me,
I can't imagine life without you…
Since our forever and always,
Doesn't have an expiration date.

The days that we're apart,
A melancholy tune...
Comes from my heart,
Letting you know...
That you are missed,
For you're one of a kind.

A life without you,
Would be very dull...
For you help me see the light,
When things go dark.

The days that we see each other,
Are my all time favorite days...
For I never want them to end,
Since our love is true.

My heart aches to be with you,
Spending all the time I can...
In your comforting embrace,
For you're my one and only.

The Homely House

Even though you're in heaven,
The house still feels like home...
For it's where you raised me,
With love and care.

When the time comes,
To leave this house that's a home,
My heart won't be ready...
For your presence will,
Always linger there.
After you passed away,
Life got harder to face...
For my heart began to ache,
To see you again.

You're an angel of God that walked the earth,
Before you had to leave for heaven...
You left a mark on the hearts of many people,
So you'll always be remembered and never forgotten.

Saying goodbye to this house that's a home,
Is much more difficult than I could of imagined...
For it's like losing a major part of me,
Even though I know I'll always have the memories.

Even though you're in heaven,
The house still feels like home...
For it's where you raised me,
With love and care.

Locked Out

The house we lived in,
You turned into a home...
Making each day alive,
Feel like a blessing.

As I leave this house,
That you raised me in...
My heart is heavy,
For your presence lingers...
In this lovely place,
Even though I'm locked out now.

With my heavy heart I try to smile,
Letting each memory created...
Lead me in the right direction,
For even though the house is gone...
I'm thankful for the life our home let me have.
Saying goodbye to the place called home,
Was like taking out a piece of my heart...
Placing it by the front door of this special place.
I may not be able to see it now,
But saying goodbye to my home—
Is making me a stronger person...
For I know that you were the reason,
That the house became home.

The house we lived in,
You turned into a home...
Making each day alive,
Feel like a blessing.

Stress Relief

It's time to take life,
One day at a time...
For it's vital to not rush,
If we don't want to miss things.

As life passes by memories are created,
Since they're the picture book...
Of each life that's lived.
Time moves faster than we may think,
So it's requested that we make the most...
Out of our lives because a mark is made,
That will remain on the hearts of those we knew.

We all have a life to live here on Earth,
Before the time comes to go home to Christ...
For he gave everyone's life a purpose.

Just take life one day at a time,
For it'll help relieve stress...
Since tomorrow may never come,
Which makes the past and today...
A beautiful gift to cherish,
No matter what events occurred.

Life will not always be easy so it's important,
To always lean on God letting him guide you...
For in every season he'll always be by your side,
Even when you feel like he's not.

The Light in my Heart

The light in my heart,
Will continue to shine...
For you helped me see,
The good in the world.

The light in my heart will never be dimmed,
For you made me understand that when times get dark...
The light will be able to shine at its brightest.

The light in my heart helps keep sadness...
From permanently staying,
Since happiness comes after tears are shed...
Allowing my heart to be mended.

Life may be harder without you here,
But I know that you're in heaven holding my hand...
Reminding me that no matter what battles I face,
I'll never be alone because heaven and earth...
Are looking out for me through God's grace.

Before you passed away you helped me see,
The difference between right and wrong...
Along with the difference between,
The light and darkness of life...
For you wanted me to know,
That you'll always be with me.

A Never Ending Love

The love I have for you is never ending.

Finding true love in this world extremely difficult,
Since when a love is true it ends up finding you...
When you least expect it making the wait worth it.

Life has cold and difficult seasons,
Along with warm and beautiful ones...
Making you and I stronger,
By cherishing the good times...
While learning from the storms,
That happen to come our way.

The love I have for you is never ending.

Love is shown in more way than one,
For the heart sees a love that's pure...
When words and actions meet,
Since the world has empty promises...
That are made by many people,
Which requires the heart...
To pay attention to someone's actions,
Instead of only listening to what's said.

When a love that's genuine decides to find you,
It'll sweep you off your feet making your life better...
For when a love is true it lasts forever and always,
Instead of a temporary time because true love never ends.

The love I have for you is never ending.

A Wounded Warrior

I'm on my deathbed now,
Although I guess I always was...
For life constantly tried to break me,
Which made me lose my mind.

The life I was living...
Was one full of pain,
Making me a wounded warrior...
Wondering what I did wrong,
Just wanting to belong...
Since I felt so out of place,
I thought I lost the race.

My heart and soul,
Seemed to be on track...
For they were honest and true,
Which is why they lead me to you.

My time on earth was lived,
With passion and compassion...
Hoping one day someone,
Would look into my eyes...
Then hold me to tell me,
They knew I wasn't fine...
For I was missing your grace,
Until I finally gave you my heart.

Now that my life on earth is ending,
The mark that I'm leaving on people I knew,
Will carry on through memories...
That they decide to share or reflect on.

The Hopeful World

Living in a world full of love...
Is peaceful and healing,
For the heart and soul...
Helping people see,
The beauty in everything.

Living in a world full of hate,
Causes pain in the heart and soul...
For they long for peace,
Instead of violence.

The world we live in,
If full of hate...
Mixed with love,
Allowing our minds...
To see the difference,
Between right and wrong...
For our heart and soul,
Need guidance from the mind...
In order to fully blossom,
From life's sun and rain.

Individually people have the power,
To fill the world with hate or love...
It's up to all of us though,
Whether the world has more—
Peace or violence in it...
Since each person leaves a mark,
That can not be silenced.

My Brain and Its Thoughts

The thoughts in my mind,
Have a way of helping...
My heart and soul,
See the light in the darkness.

The thoughts in my mind,
Sometimes get tempered with...
By the world around me,
For people have always tried...
To tell me what to say or do,
But I'll always stay true...
To the person I am,
While accepting criticism.

God has a plan that's greater,
Than everyone else's desires...
In this place called earth,
For the lord is our shepherd.

My thoughts tend to,
Keep me awake some nights...
For I must reflect on my past,
To prepare for my future...
Since I grow and bloom,
From every life event.

The thoughts in my mind,
Have a way of helping...
My heart and soul,
See the light in the darkness.

True Love Will Never End

Every breath of mine,
Gets taken away...
When you are near,
For my love for you...
Is greater than,
You'll ever know.

You make my heart full,
Filling my soul...
With a never ending joy,
Even during life's storms...
For I know times may be tough,
But I'll never be alone.

We walk hand in hand,
Making the most...
Out of our time together,
For we don't always...
Get to see each other,
Until one day...
We get our own place,
Turning it into a home.

No amount of time given to us,
Will ever be enough...
For our love story,
Is one that's never ending...
For heart will always be yours,
Since I'm in love with you...
Along with every second,
That I spend by your side.

The Symphony of Life

Heart beat by heart beat,
Breath by breath...
My life's symphony,
Begins to play.

When a smile is on my face,
The frown begins to hibernate...
Until things get hard to handle,
For the journey of life isn't meant...
To be something easy to conquer,
Since the ups and downs...
Are meant to teach and help me,
Have a better and brighter future.

Some events that occur,
Are impossible to understand...
While others are easier to comprehend.

Every day may not be enjoyable,
But each day alive is a gift...
For another day on earth,
Allows me to lend a hand...
To those in need while showing them,
That even when the lights are out,
There's always light to be found...
Even if it's hard to see,
For God is always holding our hand.

Heart beat by heart beat,
Breath by breath...
My life's symphony,
Begins to play.

A Garden of Hope

The seasons of life,
Provide nutrients for the heart...
Allowing the soul to bloom.

With each raindrop,
And each ray of sunlight...
A garden hope begins to grow.

The seasons of life,
Bring new challenges...
Allowing memories to form.

We must not walk by sight,
For God will guide us...
Since he's our shepherd.

With every new day,
Comes a new beginning...
Allowing us to see clearly,
While we walk in our faith.

The seasons of life,
May be hard to understand...
For God has a plan,
That's slowly unraveling.

With each raindrop,
And each ray of sunlight...
A garden hope begins to grow.

A Love That Remains

Some people say true love...
Doesn't exist,
Since they haven't found it.

Finding true love,
Will seem impossible...
Until you stop searching,
Since it's meant to find you.

Some people say that love,
Happens to be blind...
But it sees everything clearly,
For the heart and soul...
Work with the mind,
To turn two hearts into one.

If true love didn't exist,
Then why would there be...
People that have found,
Their one and only?
True love is a real thing,
It just takes the right person...
To make it believable,
For sometimes it's easy to hide...
Behind a wall that the heart built,
Out of pain and suffering.

When you fall in love,
With the right person...
Everything will make sense,
For you'll be soulmates.

The Daily Chapter

Breath in,
Breath out...
It's a new day.

A new day means,
That a new chapter...
Of your life has started,
So you have a new beginning.

Live for today,
Instead of...
Keeping the past,
On a constant replay.

It's vital to reflect on yesterday,
For it'll help you grow...
As you live in the moment,
While preparing for tomorrow.

Every single day,
Is your day...
So make the most,
Out of your time.

Breath in,
Breath out...
It's a new day.

A Gift From God

The pain felt in my soul,
Comes from within...
My aching heart.

God has given me you,
And your loving embrace...
Heals my melancholy feelings.

You're a man,
With a pure heart,
And honest soul...
That knows me better,
Than anyone else.
You're my forever and always,
The hand I'll never let go of...
For you have all of me,
You're my one and only.
Life without you,
Would be empty...
For you're the reason,
My heart keeps its beat.

God has a plan,
For the two of us...
Which I know is beautiful.
Life may not always,
Go the way we wish it would...
But with God by our side,
We can make it through...
All of the hills and valleys,
That come our way.

See You Soon

You left earth,
To join God...
In heaven.

I didn't want to say goodbye,
So instead I said farewell...
I'll see you soon.

My heart broke...
When you took,
Your final breath...
And as I said farewell,
Melancholy feelings arrived...
For I was scared,
To live this life without you.

The memories we made,
Will never begin to dim...
For your legacy,
Will always live on.

Life here on earth,
Without you here...
Will always be hard,
For I miss you dearly.

My guardian angel,
Thank you for everything...
I wouldn't be who I am,
If it wasn't for you.

The Moon and The Sun

The moon begins,
To dance with the stars...
While the sun hides,
Waiting for tomorrow...
To finally arrive.

As nighttime changes,
Into daylight...
The moon kisses the sun,
To remind her she's loved.

The people of the world,
Are on a journey...
That doesn't always,
Have the best weather.

Through the ups and downs,
Of the life we live...
There will always be light,
For the darkness...
Has less power,
Since the light of God...
Will always shine,
Showing us we're not alone.

Even though the hours of the day,
Fade away...
Into the end of time,
Our legacy will forever remain.

Our Love Story

When you're around,
My heart fails to frown...

When you have to leave,
My heart grows weary...
As I miss you more,
With every second...

For we say goodnight,
And see you soon...

After every time,
We see each other...

But a day will come,
Where we never...
Have to say goodbye,
Since our love is true...

God has given me you,
My soulmate and better half...

I'll always be yours,
Through the thick and thin...
In sickness and in health.

Our love story has no ending...
It's one that will go on,
Forever and Always.

Joining Jesus In Heaven

If heaven had visiting hours,
I'm not sure...
I'd know just what to say.

If heaven had visiting hours...
I'd stay for as long as I could,
Giving you one more hug...
Making the most,
Out of these precious moments.

If heaven had visiting hours,
Earth's rain showers...
Wouldn't seem as bad.

You were an angel on earth,
That eventually had to go...
Join Jesus in heaven,
To become my guardian angel.

If heaven had visiting hours,
I'm not sure...
I'd know just what to say,
For it would take my breath away.

Even though time was cut short,
The memories we made...
Will live on forever.

The Warrior In Your Heart

Melancholy feelings,
Can get overwhelming...
For life doesn't always,
Go the way we wish it would.

Happiness and sadness,
Are important for the soul...
To know and experience,
For they go hand in hand.

Without hardships and pain,
Then happiness and comfort...
Would become less powerful and meaningful.

It can get hard to see,
The beauty of life at times...
But we must remember that better days are ahead.

You're a warrior and a survivor...
You're a hero to someone,
For you've impacted lives.
The life you live,
Is a precious one...
Never let anyone tell you otherwise.

When the melancholy feelings,
Try to take over your heart and mind...
Just reach out your hand...
You'll never have,
To fight your battles alone,
For you are cared for.

We Came A Long Way

Bad days are the storms,
That we go through...
In order to get to,
Rainbows and brighter days.

The past may not be,
Something pleasant...
But we must not forget,
Where we once came from...
For it has shaped us,
Into who we are now.

Through the sun and rain...
Through smiles and frowns,
Through the ups and downs...
We've come a long,
Long way...
So we mustn't quit now.

Use the storm as a guide,
To later find sunshine...
Since the rain will,
Eventually end...
Allowing us to be thankful,
For all that we have...
Instead of becoming greedy.

Bad days are the storms,
That we go through...
In order to get to,
Rainbows and brighter days.

Invisible

As my tears hit the ground,
I wonder if anyone sees...
Or if my cries make me,
Become invisible to others.

My heart is aching,
And you can see it...
From each tear,
That falls from my eyes.

I've had good days,
And bad days...
But they both,
Shaped me into...
The person,
That I am today.

As my tears hit the ground,
I wonder if anyone sees...
Or if my cries make me,
Become invisible to others.

There are days,
Where my smile means nothing...
Which is why it's vital,
To pay attention to my eyes.

The pain in my heart,
Won't last forever...
For the storm is there,
To help me grow...
Into who I'm meant to be.

The sun will shine again,
And when it does...
I'll be stronger than I was,
In the season of rain.

As my tears hit the ground,
I wonder if anyone sees...
Or if my cries make me,
Become invisible to others.

I am who I am,
And I'll always be me...
Even when I'm not confident,
For I have my flaws...
And I know life won't go,
As planned...
But,
I have the Lord to thank...
For another day alive,
No matter what happens.

Facing Reality

My heart is like a canvas,
For everything I go through...
Paints my heart,
Different shades and colors.

My soul is like the stars,
For there are times...
The pathway needs,
More light...
In order to lead me,
The proper direction in life.

My mind is like a rollercoaster,
For some thoughts last...
Longer than others,
Going up and down.

My eyes are like a waterfall when I begin to cry,
For the tears don't hold back at all.

When facing reality,
I must remember...
That my dreams don't,
Have to remain dreams.

My heart, soul, and mind...
All work together,
To make sure I live life to the fullest...
Instead of letting it,
Pass me by a day at a time.

Get Back Up

I fall down sometimes,
But God tells me...
I need to get back up,
For my story's not done yet.

You will also fall down,
And that's okay...
For the storms in life,
Make us appreciate...
The good stuff,
That comes our way.

Whether you believe this,
Or whether you don't...
Your life truly matters,
And I hope that...
No matter how hard,
Your life gets...
That you'll keep fighting,
For it won't be stormy in life forever.

We are all leaving our mark,
On the people around us...
And you'll forever be loved,
Never let anyone tell you different.

Taking A Breath of Fresh Air

Take a deep breath,

And step outside.

Whether it be,

Morning...

Noon,

Or night...

Take a look,

At the sky.

Use this moment,

Of fresh air...

To release the tension,

You may be feeling.

Take a deep breath,

And whisper a prayer...

Because in time,

Everything will...

Fall into place,

And be alright.

Close your eyes,

And imagine...

The scent of roses,

Or...

The sound of the ocean,

And remember...

This is a fight,

That you'll never face alone.

Find a moment in your day,

And use it just for you...

Relax and allow your world,

To stop rushing...

Just for a second,

So that way you can...

Take your much needed deep breath.

The Remembrance Candle

Light a candle,
In remembrance of me.

Cry if you need to cry,
Scream and shout...
If it helps you grieve,
Just let it all out...
Light a candle,
In remembrance of me.

As much as it pains me...
To see you hurting,
Since I'm no longer...
Physically here,
I need you to know...
I'll always watch over you,
From up above.

I'll forever be with you,
No matter the distance...
So when your heart aches,
Because you miss me...
Light a candle,
In remembrance of me.

You'll see me again someday,
But until then keep your head up...
And never forget,
That I'll always love you.

Light a candle,
In remembrance of me.

Speechless

As I try to speak,
Words don't always…
Decide to come out.

Whether I'm speechless,
Or not…
My actions will show,
What my heart's…
Trying to say.

I'm not alone,
And neither are you…
There's people around,
That care for you.

Don't focus on,
What everyone thinks…
When you could be,
Focusing on…
Making the most,
Out of this day.

As I try to speak,
Words don't always…
Decide to come out.

What's your heart,
Trying to tell…
The world?

The Struggling Soul

My heart is heavy,
With pain and suffering.

My soul is trying,
To remain hopeful...
For an era has ended,
But the memories remain.

My heart is heavy,
While my soul struggles...
Through the pain and rain.

I'm not alone,
With Christ guiding me.

I'm not alone,
For the love of my life...
Is holding my hand,
Making sure I don't lose faith.

I'm not alone,
And I don't have to...
Let my tears be silent anymore.

My heart is heavy tonight,
But beautiful memories...
Come from stormy nights,
And early sunrises.

Our Life

Inside your arms,
Is where I belong...

With you is where,
I'd rather be...

Right now the distance is far,
But one day it won't be...

For I love you,
Always and forever...

Our love is real,
So whenever you're near...
I'm finally home,
Where I should be.

What we have,
Will never die...
Since God gave us,
One another.

We'll live our life on earth,
Together hand in hand...

We'll dance,
In heaven together...
When the time comes.

We individually have flaws,
But together we're perfect.

We Mustn't Forget

When my heart and soul,
Look at the stars...
They see their beauty.
When my mind,
Looks at the stars...
It begins to study them.

No two stars are the same,
Just like us people...
We'll have similarities,
But there will always...
Be differences.
There's inner beauty,
And there's appearances...
But look for the beauty,
That comes from within...
For looks can be deceiving.

People are like stars,
For sometimes their light…
May be harder to see,
For we're going through...
Different seasons in life.

We mustn't forget,
That just because...
Our pathway may not be,
Fully lit up...
God is guiding us,
Through every step...
Never abandoning us.

A Heart With A Wish

A wish is something,
That your heart will make...
Whether it be,
While you're awake...
Or whether it be,
While you're asleep.

We all have a wish,
That lives inside us...
That wants to be granted,
But sometimes wishes...
Take time to grant.

Even if...
Your wish doesn't,
Come true today...
There's still a chance,
That your wish or dream...
Will be reality,
In the morning.

Let your heart and soul,
Be led by God's grace...
For he'll always,
Have your back...
Even when you run,
Away for a little while.

If you had one wish,
What would it be...
And why?

A Poem to the Love of My Life

My heart has been,
As delicate as a Rose...
And as fragile,
As a picture frame.

I may be human,
But I'm a flower in God's garden...
And each day that I'm given,
Is captured in a photo,
That my guardian angels...
Put into a picture frame,
To help make distance bearable.

I've experienced loss,
I've experienced joy...
And I now know,
What true love really is.

I've had role models,
That have shown me...
What love is,
And what soulmates are...
But I guess I needed to wait,
To fully understand...
Because it was part of God's plan,
To bring us together.

When God brought you,
Into this life of mine...
I knew he had a special reason,
And that everything would be okay.

So when I met you—
I took a deep breath,
And I smiled...
As I looked into your eyes.

Now that we've made,
So many memories together...
Sometimes I have to look down,
To keep myself from crying...
Because our love is so beautiful,
And precious to me.

I may not know,
What God has planned...
For the future,
But I look forward...
To spending it,
With you by my side.

I love you,
Is more...
Than a phrase to me.

I love you,
Is more...
Than a simple feeling.

When I say I love you,
I mean it...
With my heart and soul.

When I say I love you,
I mean it...
More than I'll ever be able to show.

Forever and always,
Is more than a time frame...
For it reminds us,
That no matter what happens...
We'll get through it together,
Hand in hand.

If you step outside,
And look up at the stars...
You'll be reminded,
That I'll always love you...
And that I'll forever,
Be by your side.

Signs From Heaven

I look for you,
And call out for you...
The heavens hear my cry,
My plea to see you again...
One last time.

There's no visiting hours up in heaven,
So I have to wait till my time comes...
To be reunited with you.

As I look for you,
And call out for you...
Silence fills my ears,
While the hope in my heart remains...
Since I'll never forget you.

You and God worked hard,
When it came to taking care of me...
And making sure,
That everything was alright.

As I look for you,
And call out for you...
The heavens hear my cry,
My plea to see you again...
One last time,
So I receive the signs...
That you send down,
From up above...
To help me clearly see,
That you'll forever...
Be holding my hand.

Try

When you look at my smile,
The pain may not...
Be revealed right away.

When you look at my eyes,
You see my heart and soul...
Which ends up showing you,
The pain I feel inside.

I try to always smile,
I try to always be strong...
But even strong people,
Break down at some point.

From one quick glance,
You won't see...
Everything that,
I've been through.

When you take the time,
To get to know me...
You'll understand,
Why I am who I am.

First To Last

From our first breath,
To our first words...
We start to blossom,
Into who we're meant to be.

Through the smiles...
Through the laughter,
And through the tears...
Of sorrow and melancholy,
We continue to grow.

From the moment we're born,
To the moment we die...
We leave a legacy and mark,
On this place called earth.

When we breath,
Our final breath...
We leave the place,
That we called home.

Our home was where,
Our hearts...
Decided to take us.

We leave earth,
To join the father...
Up in heaven,
To watch over loved ones.

Is Love Blind?

I've been told,
That love is blind.

I've been shown,
That love is seen...
With the heart and mind,
Not with the human eye.

If love is blind,
Why is it...
So powerful?

If love is blind,
How come we fall so hard...
When we find our soulmate?

How is love blind?
I've been dying to know...
For what I've been told,
About how love is blind...
Seemed true at the time,
Until I fell in love.

After falling in love,
I realized the truth...
That Love is the furthest,
Thing from being blind.

When love is real,
It always gets revealed...
In a matter of time.

Heaven Called

When heaven called you,
To leave this world...
My heart began to ache.

When heaven took,
You away from me...
I felt lost and afraid.
I needed more time,
I wasn't ready...
To say goodbye to you.

The day you passed away,
I lost a major part of me...
Or so I thought,
For the longest time.

After some time went by,
I came to realize...
That you'll always,
Be here with me...
Even when it feels,
Like you're far away.

I can't visit,
My guardian angel...
But I can pray.

One day I'll see you again,
And I know you'd want me...
To be strong for you,
And keep fighting...
To stay alive,
For you want me to live...
My life to its fullest.

My heart still aches,
Without you here...
But I'm stronger now,
Than when you first left...
Since I know you're near.

A Story Left Behind

The past shows,
That life...
Hasn't always,
Been easy.

The present shows,
That I've grown...
And come long way,
From where I used to be.

The past turned me,
Into a warrior...
And a survivor.

The future is unknown,
But no matter what...
I'll use my past,
Along with...
Each new moment,
To live life.

The past is a mark,
That I left on the world.

The present is a mark,
That I'm leaving,
On the world.

The future is a mark,
That I will make...
On the world.

This mark I'm leaving,
Is my story and legacy…
That I hope,
Helps at least one person.

When I breath my final breath,
My story will be complete…
Thank you to everyone,
Who made this journey…
One worthwhile.

The Key to My Heart

The sound of your voice,
Calms my fears.

Your embrace,
Makes me feel...
Like I'm finally home.

When I look into your eyes,
I know that I'm safe...
And truly loved.

Without you,
My heart would ache...
For I'd be homeless,
Since home is where...
My heart leads me,
And it brought me to you.

A world without you,
Would be dark and gloomy.

I've missed you,
In the past.

I miss you,
When we're apart.

You hold the only key,
To my heart.

You knocked down,
The walls that I built...
In an attempt to protect,
My heart and soul.

I've been hurt before,
But with you...
I don't have to worry,
Because I know...
That you mean what you say,
For your words...
Along with your actions,
Show me that our love...
Is forever,
And always.

The Past Meets Today

Each star in the sky,
Is a piece of the past...
That leads us to the future.

The moon and the sun,
Dance in the sky.

From darkness,
To daylight...
We see that life,
Sometimes gets rough...
But there will always,
Be light...
Even if,
It's hard to see.

The sky and the ground,
Spin round and round.

I wonder if I'll wake up,
In the morning.

During this day,
I'll use the reflection,
Of my past...
To help me through,
Whatever comes my way today.

So I ask myself,
And I ask you...
What will you do,
To change the world?

Look to The Stars

The stars shine down,
To remind me...
Of my past to prepare me,
For what the future holds.

The stars shine down,
To remind me...
That I'll never be alone.

The stars shine down,
To remind me...
That even in the dark,
A light still shines even if it's dim.

My heart and soul,
Must look to the stars...
And ask God,
To help us through this day.

When the day is done,
And the stars come out...
I must take a moment,
Of pure silence...
And thank the lord,
For the day we had.

Now when my time,
Comes to go to heaven...
Lift your head up,
And remember...
To look at the stars,
For I'll always be with you.

Colliding Hearts

The sound of your voice,
Comforts my soul.

When you whisper,
It gives me chills...
For the stress of the day,
Somehow disappears.

When you're near,
I always feel...
Like I'm home.

The touch of your hand,
Makes fear run and hide...
For it knows,
Our hearts have collided.

When God,
Brought us together...
He turned you and I,
Into one.

No amount of distance,
Can keep us apart...
For our love is true.

Memorial Day

Those who have fallen,
Those who have fought...
And to those who fight,
For this country...
You deserve,
The greatest thanks.

Our freedom,
Is far from free...
For lives were lost,
And lives are risked.

You defend us,
And all that we know.

I hope you know,
How much...
You're appreciated,
Even when it seems...
Like the world doesn't care.

To the fallen,
To those out of battle...
And to those fighting,
Thank you for everything.

On this Memorial Day,
Take some time to thank a veteran...
And spend some time with those you love,
For you never know how much time is left.

One Day You'll Understand

Falling in love,
Must happen naturally.

Forced feelings,
Won't get you far...
It'll only break your heart.

Falling in love,
Must happen naturally.

Through the highs and the lows,
Through the laughter and tears...
Always lend an ear,
No matter how busy you may be.

Falling in love,
Must happen naturally.

Once you've found the one,
You may feel like it's a dream,
But when you fall in love...
And it all happens naturally...
You'll understand why I say,
True love will never end.

Sparrows and Blue Jays

The sparrows dance in the evening,
As the blue jays sing at sunrise.

My heart beats,
As your soul sings...
For love has made us,
Into one.

As the sparrows dance in the evening,
The owls watch...
Making sure peace remains.

One breath at a time,
One step per moment...
Taking life as it comes,
Learning from the past...
While creating memories,
And leaving a mark here on earth.

My heart beats,
As your soul sings...
For love has made us,
Into one.

As the sparrows dance in the evening,
It shows us that this love of ours...
Will never fade.

From when we first met,
To our first date...
Up until now so much has happened—
And I just want to say that I love you my dear.

The sparrows dance in the evening,
As the blue jays sing at sunrise...
Whether it be rain or shine.

We fell in love,
Through the sun and the rain...
So in some ways,
We're like the sparrows and blue jays.

I'm Sorry

I feel lost.

I feel useless.

My depression,

Is trying to come back.

I'm going down this painful road,

And I want it to end.

I'm sorry for being a burden,

I'm sorry for not being perfect…

I'm sorry for disappointing you,

I'm sorry for caring so deeply…

I'm sorry for everything,

Even for breathing.

I wonder...

When I'm eventually gone,

Who would even notice.

Will I Ever be Good Enough?

I'm trying to talk to you,
But if feels useless...
Since you never listen.

I'm trying to talk to you,
But why should I bother...
You don't care anyway.

I'm trying to talk to you,
But I probably shouldn't...
Since I mean nothing to you.

I'm trying to talk to you,
But I'm wasting my breath...
You don't want me around.

I gave you my heart,
But I started regretting that...
The day your true colors showed.

I'm about to give up on you...
And when I do,
Don't start to care...
Or attempt to listen.

When I'm done,
There is no going back...
Because I'll be gone for good,
I can promise you that...
I'm sorry I wasn't good enough.

In God's Eyes

There's a mirror on the wall,
And I've started to avoid...
Looking in it at night,
For I have a hard time...
Seeing beauty,
Within my reflection.

I'm losing confidence daily,
And I'm not proud of my body...
But I'm trying to be a better me.

So in the morning I'll look,
In this mirror...
And make eye contact,
With the reflection of me...
Motivating myself,
To make the most out of the day.

I'm learning,
That my flaws and imperfections...
Are beautiful in God's eyes,
And his opinion matters most.

An Explanation From The Heart

I dress the way,
That I want to dress...
Whether it be—
Casual or fancy,
With or without makeup...
Nothing can stop me,
From staying true to who I am.

My personality better explains,
Who I truly am...
So don't rely on my looks,
To tell my life story.

Looks can tell you,
A little bit about me...
But until you take time,
To actually get to know me...
You'll never fully understand,
Who I am and why.

I don't come with,
A movie trailer...
Or book summary,
Even though I use social media.

So unless you're willing,
To put in effort...
You'll never know,
Even half of what...
Makes me the person,
Standing before you today.

Soaring High Above the Clouds

Like a bird I soar,
High above the clouds...
Occasionally resting,
Before my next flight.

I once was a small caterpillar...
That faced storms and difficulties,
Before turning into a butterfly...
And when I finally got wings of my own,
I had spread them...
Joining the birds,
On the journey in the sky.

Time is limited,
And the clock is running out...
So I'm not quite sure,
How much longer...
I'll get to enjoy,
This beautiful place called earth.

When I must leave,
I'll take my wings to heaven...
And continue to keep a watchful eye,
On those that made life worth living.

Giving God My Heart

When I became weak,
I finally gave God...
My entire heart,
Instead of trying to hide...
My sorrows and flaws.

In this life of mine,
It took a while...
For me to see,
That God loves all of me.

I've come close to leaving earth,
Because my melancholy feelings...
Had gotten to be to much,
But finally I got help...
And I started to see clearly,
That everything had to have happened...
For a reason.

My rough patches,
Brought me closer to God...
And they showed me,
That it's more than okay to be me.

The Power of Words and Actions

If you don't practice,
The things you teach...
Isn't it misleading?

If you don't practice,
What you're preaching...
Then what's the point,
Of sharing the message?

You share your knowledge,
With the world...
But why,
What's the point?
The phrases your lips speak,
Become less powerful...
If your heart isn't in it.

If you want to be understood,
You should allow your words...
To turn into actions,
For they're the proof...
That eventually shows,
If you're honest or not.

Do you practice,
What you preach...
Or do you pretend to be,
Someone else abandoning yourself?

If you don't practice,
What you teach and preach...
Does it break your heart,
Knowing you're hiding?

If you have something to say,
Don't be afraid to let it out...
If you want to do something,
Then go and do it.

Stay true to yourself,
Because in the end...
You'll be glad you did.

By Your Side

You're no longer here,
So I shed a tear...
Wishing you were near.

No more jokes,
No more story time...
No more hugs,
No more disagreements...
On who loves who more,
For everything is now...
Only a memory,
That was made.

You're no longer here,
So I shed a tear...
Wishing you were near.

There's a piece of me,
That will always miss you...
But there's also a piece,
That is glad...
That you're in heaven,
With God looking down...
On those you loved,
And left behind.

You're no longer here,
So I shed a tear...
Wishing you were near.

If heaven allowed visitors,
I know I'd run to you...
But since it doesn't,
I'll have to wait...
For my time to come,
And when that day arrives...
I hope you know,
That I'll be by your side.

You're no longer here,
So I shed a tear...
Wishing you were near.

The Tears That Come Down Like Rain

The rain,
Is like our tears.

The rain can cause,
The world to be happy...
But it can also cause,
The world a great deal of pain.

Our tears,
Is like the rain.

After the storm,
The sun always..
Manages to find its way out,
From behind the clouds.

Our fears and tears,
Our joy and laughter...
Build up,
Throughout the years...
Teaching us,
Everything we must know.

In the beginning,
All the way...
Until the end,
We have a choice to make.

Will our rain and tears,
Allow us to drown...
Or will we trust the Lord,
With our heart and soul?

A List of Lessons

You taught me and the family,
A long list of things...
Through your words,
And everything you did.

Home is where,
Your heart leads you...
And God brought you here,
To a place that became...
Your earthly home,
Where this family grew.

Because of you,
I'll always remember...
Who I am,
And where I came from.

You're my hero and lifesaver,
Who made each day...
Full of smiles and excitement,
Till the day God called you...
Away from earth,
To your heavenly home.

With each passing day,
You always cross my mind...
Making me wish,
I could travel back in time.

I'll always remember you,
For you left major footprints...
On this heart of mine,
Thank you for being you...
And for helping me become,
The person I am today!

The Beauty of Time

Time is beautiful.

Time heals,
But it also...
Causes tears.

Time allows us,
To remember the past...
Even though,
Sometimes it hurts.

Time allows us,
To live in the now...
As we make our mark,
On the world.

Time allows us,
To prepare...
For the future,
That will arrive soon.

Time heals,
But it also...
Causes tears.

Time encourages us,
To be thankful...
For everything we have,
And everyone who leaves…
Footprints on our heart.

Time is beautiful.

As The Wind Blows

As the wind blows,
The wolves howl...
And the sound of crows,
Echo in the woods.

As the day goes by,
I begin to wonder...
How much time,
I have left.

My heart and soul,
Play a song...
That most tune out,
While others add harmony...
Trying not to miss a moment,
Of this piece.

As I put one foot,
In front of the other...
Taking life,
One breath at a time...
I think about,
You and I.

As the wind blows,
Everyday eventually ends...
Making us have hope for tomorrow,
While being thankful for today.

Writing Your Name In The Sand

Sparks fly,
As lightning bugs...
Soar in the night sky.

Sparks fly,
Between you and I...
Making my heart and soul,
Feel happy and alive.

Being with you,
Has made me understand...
Why I had to wait,
For true love to find me.
God's has a plan,
And it is grand...
So I'll write your name,
In the sand.
The world needs,
To comprehend...
That I'm happily taken,
Forever and always.
I want you to know,
I love you...
With my heart and soul.

Sparks fly,
In more ways than one...
And I'm glad that God,
Has given me you.
Sparks fly,
And time can't...
Stop this heart of mine,
From loving you...
With all that I am,
Till death do us part.

Roses from The Heart

GIVING YOUR WOMAN A RED ROSE,

REMINDS HER OF YOUR LOVE…

GIVING HER A BLUE ROSE,

TELLS HER YOU MISS HER…

GIVING HER A WHITE ROSE,

PROMISES HER FOREVER…

AND GIVING HER A BLACK ROSE,

TELLS HER THAT YOU NEVER…

WANT TO LOSE HER.

Spending Forever With You

You say you care,
Like love is in the air...
But words and actions,
Are two separate things...
That happen to go,
Hand in hand...
And that's something,
We mustn't forget.

We need forget material things,
For they aren't as important...
As making time for one another.

Without you,
Any belief of forever...
Just disappears,
Into thin air.

If you ask me to leave,
I eventually will...
Slowly but surely,
Hoping you would...
Change your mind,
And ask me to stay.

You have my heart,
You have my trust...
I've given you my life,
I love you for you...
With all that I am,
So I hope you'll always...
Decide to keep me by your side.

I Love You

The light in your eyes,

Is like the sun in the sky...

Or the stars when they shine.

The light in your eyes,

Is so bright & beautiful...

And I hope you know,

That I love you for you.

Without you by my side,

The world would go dark...

Breaking my heart.

What Is True Love?

True love doesn't end with a kiss.
True love doesn't expire...
True love lasts,
Forever and always.

Living happily ever after,
Reminds us that...
Life has just,
Fully begun.

Our journey,
Is a love story...
That will go on,
Even after...
Our time on earth,
Has come to an end.

True love is powerful and turns,
Two hearts into one.
True love doesn't end with a kiss,
For true love never ends.

What Can Be Seen?

When I look,
Into your eyes...
I can see where,
The sun rises.

When I look,
Into your eyes...
I can see where,
The moon tries to hide.

When I look,
Into your eyes...
I can see the light,
That shines from within.

When I look,
Into your eyes...
I can see the lord,
Has touched your soul.

When I look,
Into your eyes...
I can see that with you,
Is where I belong.

It's Time You Know My Battle Scars

My eyes reveal what I feel inside,
While my smile remains in tact.

I don't wear,
My heart and soul...
On my sleeve,
For everyone to see.

I don't break down...
In front of everyone,
So if I show you...
The hurt that I feel inside,
I hope you won't run and hide.

When I let you in,
And give you the chance...
To know my battle scars,
It's because I trust you.

Yes you have to earn my trust,
And once you have it...
I hope you won't,
Take advantage of it.

I don't wear,
My heart and soul...
On my sleeve,
For everyone to see.

So if you ever lose my trust,
I highly doubt,
That you'll get it back...
But in time—
If you do end up gaining,
Some of my trust back...
Know that I'll never,
Fully let you in again.

But if you mean what you say,
And you show me how you feel...
The places we could go,
Are magical and limitless.

The Fragile Heart

Love is more,
Than these words...
That you speak.

Show me,
That what you say...
Is true.

I've been hurt,
In the past...
So I built a wall,
Around my heart.

If you tear down...
My heart's wall,
Remember that...
This heart of mine,
Is fragile...
And try not to hurt me.

Love is not blind...
At least when it's true,
So if you love someone...
Show them you do.

Stepping Into A Fairytale

I toss and turn at night,
Wondering if you're alright.

Even when you're out of sight,
You'll always be on my mind.

You're the light that shines,
So bright in my life.

A fantasy turned into reality,
The day that we met...
For I felt like I stepped,
Right into a fairytale.

God knew exactly,
When I should meet...
The love of my life,
And I'm glad...
That he made me wait,
Because he gave me you.

A Table For Two

There's a table for two,
For just me and you...
And one day,
We'll say I do.

As we walk hand in hand,
I can't stop myself...
From looking back at you.

Through rain and shine,
Day and night...
Nothing can separate,
These hearts of ours.

Saying I do is more,
Than just words we speak...
For our love is shown,
Through all that we do.

There's a table for two,
For just me and you...
For today is our day,
We have said I do.

An Anchor of Love

When you're around,
My smile is like a field...
Of flowers in full bloom.

When you're around,
Any case of the blues...
Somehow disappears.

Your love is like an anchor,
Constantly reminding me...
To never give up.

Your love is like an anchor,
Reminding me that life is beautiful...
And that it's worth living.

Home is where,
Your heart leads you...
And God made my heart,
Lead me to you.

Inside your arms,
Is where I can say...
That I'm finally home.

The Forever Child

My eyes are a mirror,
For they reveal…
What I feel inside,
Whether it be…
Happiness,
Or sadness.

My heart is like a candle,

I let my light shine for Jesus…

But eventually my flame will go out,

Because the lord called me home.

My soul is like the sky,
Since I find the sun…
When I call upon the Lord,
Especially in the midst of a storm.

Jesus has my back,

For he'd never let me drown…

I just have to trust him,

With all that I am.

As I have walked this earth,
I've seen sorrow and joy…
Tears and smiles,
And hope restored.

I am a forever child,

Of the one true king…

So I give him,

My heart and soul…

And trust him,

With my life.

My walk with Jesus,
Will never end…
For no one can separate,
A father from his child.

When the Time Comes

What do you see,
When you look at me?

What do you think,
When you hear my name?

When you listen to my voice,
Do you feel inspired or lonely?

Is this life of ours,
Just a game being played...
Or is it a work of art,
That comes together with time?

I've come to realize,
That honesty and love...
Is the medicine we need,
To keep our mended hearts beating.

When the time comes,
To say farewell...
I'll make sure,
That your legacy never dies.

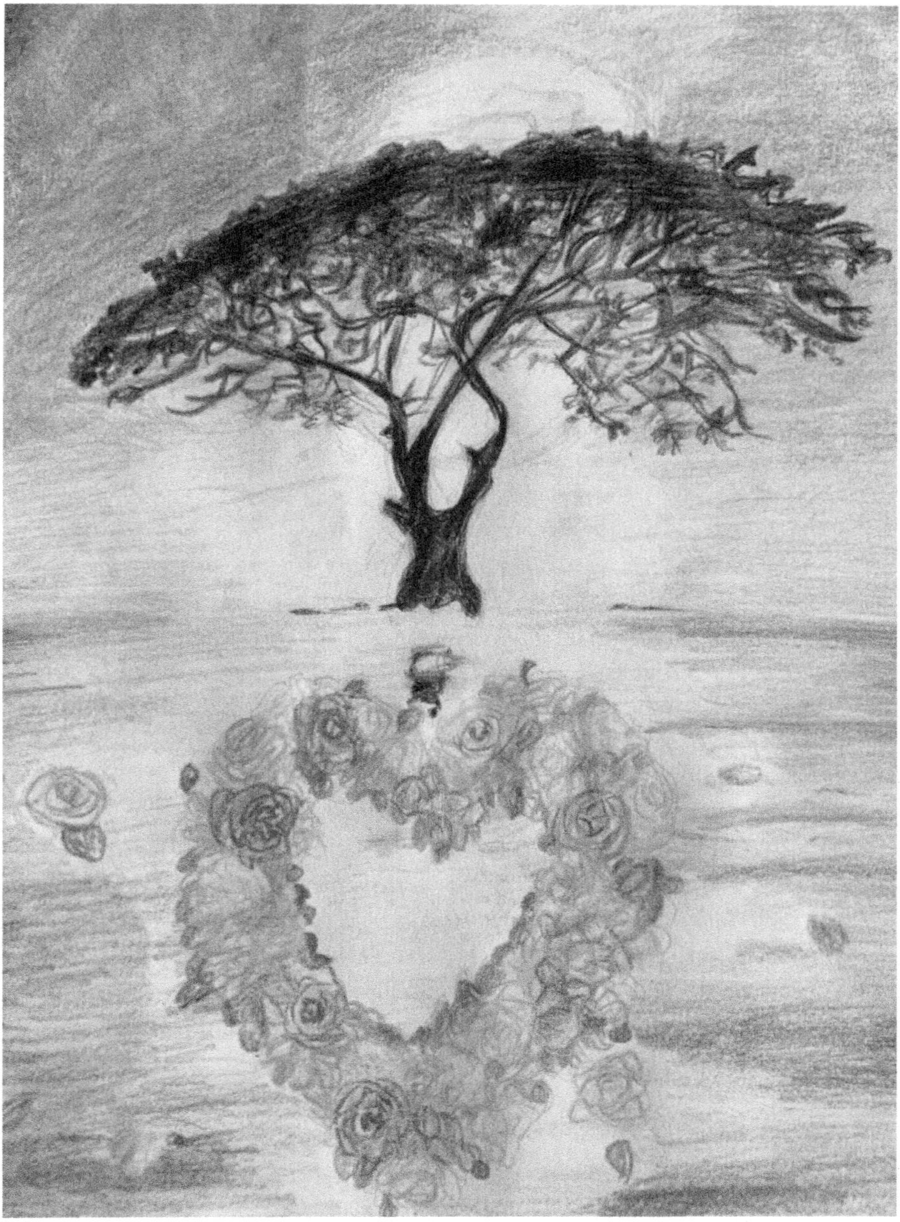

Wise Words from Owen Norris:

"Love. It's a curious state. Is it not? It can make us feel like we're on top of the world. Like we're the most amazing people on Earth and no one can take that away from us. It can make us feel like we're flying letting our bodies take us wherever it pleases. But yet love can make us feel like we're defective machines. Waiting for our makers to throw us into the flames that will destroy us. Love can make us feel like we're nothing and do not belong on this Earth. Love can often be compared to the way the rain falls from the heavens above. Times it will be calm and peaceful. It can be quite lovely. Like you falling in love for the first time. The rain matching the beat of your love infected heart as you think of your love. However rain can bring dangerous storms. Storms that bring tornados and such. Destroying homes and land. Matching the way you now feel about your former love. It can bring great floods. Sweeping away everything in front of it. Similar to the way you're crying because your love cheated on you. But do not worry for all rain must stop at one point. When that rain stops the sun your friend will come to you drying away all the rain and tears upon you. Helping you start all over again."

"I want to make a difference, feed the world, bleed so the poor don't have to, weed the wrong & seed the just. Maybe I will someday, probably not tomorrow, but it never hurts to start today. In short, to serve others is to serve myself."

*In Loving Memory of those that have passed away,
Take a moment of silence and feel their presence…
For they'll always be with you.*

About The Author

Diana Douglas is from Kent, Ohio and loves working with children. She works with children at church; and is going to college to become an Elementary school teacher and a counselor. Diana makes custom quilts (including t-shirt quilts). She attends craft shows in the fall and early winter every year selling things she has made or created. She has been sewing and quilting since she was very young because her grandmother taught her that homemade things will be treasured for a longer period of time. If something lacks the presence of the heart, more and more people will be quicker to turn away or throw something away. Whenever Diana picks up the pen, it's like a whole new world begins.

Made in the USA
Monee, IL
08 June 2023